A Heart for God

A Journey With David
From Brokenness to Wholeness

Charles P. Schmitt

Destiny Image Publishers, Inc.®
P.O. Box 310
Shippensburg, PA 17257-0310

"Speaking to the Purposes of God for this Generation
and for the Generations to Come"

ISBN 1-56043-157-1

For Worldwide Distribution
Printed in the U.S.A.

Destiny Image books are available through these fine distributors outside the United States:

Christian Growth, Inc. Jalan Kilang-Timor, Singapore 0315	Vine Christian Centre Mid Glamorgan, Wales, United Kingdom
Rhema Ministries Trading Randburg, South Africa	Vision Resources Ponsonby, Auckland, New Zealand
Salvation Book Centre Petaling, Jaya, Malaysia	WA Buchanan Company Geebung, Queensland, Australia
Successful Christian Living Capetown, Rep. of South Africa	Word Alive Niverville, Manitoba, Canada

Inside the U.S., call toll free to order:
1-800-722-6774

Our 30-Day Journey

Part One: God Prepares David, His Chosen

Part Two: God Uses David, His Chosen

A Word of Sincere Thanks

David writes, "The Lord gave the word and great was the company of women that published it" (Ps. 68:11, lit.).

I keenly sensed the presence of God as I wrote these 30 chapters on David's journey from brokenness to wholeness. I can attribute the inspiration on these pages to Him: "the Lord gave the word."

But wherever would I have been had it not been for that company of faithful women who helped to publish it? My wife Dotty, with her own achievements as an author, was my constant encouragement and most helpful critic. I owe so much to my personal secretary, Fran Ladson, as she typed, retyped, then typed yet again these chapters, incorporating into them the editing of three gifted ladies: Dr. Aija Ozolins, Linda Walker, and Virene Càrdenas. To the patient labors of Sue Morrisson I owe the final camera-ready formatting of these pages; and to both the men and women at Destiny Image I owe much—for their guidance and their final fine-tuning of these chapters for publication. To all these I give a sincere word of thanks. Thank you in Jesus' dear name!

Why David?

A study of the life of David is essential, I believe, to our proper understanding of the nature of God's redeeming and restoring grace. Few men entered the Kingdom of God with as many millstones tied about their necks as did David, son of Jesse. David was bound by a curse pronounced by God generations before his conception. His birth was shrouded in the mystery of sin and probable moral failure. His childhood was broken and flawed, according to his own pained testimony. David consequently grew up to be a very dysfunctional man. He was a failure as a husband and as a father. In his royal court, David's servants pictured him as a volcano ready to explode. His notorious guilt as an adulterer and a murderer deeply stained the sacred record; yet, in spite of it all, David rose to become one of the most intensely spiritual persons in all of Holy Scripture, second only to our Lord Jesus Christ.

David's name appears in the Word of God more than 1,150 times. The fact that he is named more often than any other patriarch, priest, prophet, king, or apostle—only our God and His Christ are named more frequently—is a clear testimony to how the Father Himself viewed David: an honored and cherished man after His own heart. David *was* a man of God. Pulling all the facts of his life together, we cannot but touch something of the revelation of God's redeeming and restoring grace. David pressed beyond his abysmal sin and failure, even beyond the severity of God's disciplines and judgments against his sin, into the very forgiveness and deliverance of God. The mercy of God came to David and redeemed him. David found and treasured the grace of God, Jehovah's covenant love, and that covenant love restored him.

The life of David, more than the life of any other Bible character, can bring hope to those bound by generational curses, to those born in sin, and to those raised in shame. David's life can inspire faith in the hearts of the dysfunctional, the failure-ridden, and the fallen. The world is full of such men and women. Consequently, we as the Church have our own share of them as well. Perhaps you, like me, are one of that needy number. This 30-day journey from brokenness to wholeness is dedicated to you. (Please take time, especially, to read the Scripture readings for each day, and to trace the geographical references on the maps in the back of your Bible.)

Through studying David's story we shall all be well able to rejoice greatly in a God who, in His covenant love, has "predestined *us* to be adopted as His sons through Jesus Christ...to the praise of His glorious grace, which He has freely given *us* in the One He loves" (Eph. 1:5-6).

Charles P. Schmitt
Immanuel's Church
Silver Spring, Maryland

David's Time Line

(Dates are approximate)

1085 BC	• David Ben Jesse's birth at Bethlehem
1068 BC	• David's anointing by Samuel (age 17)
1065 BC	• David's defeat of Goliath (age 20)
1062-1055 BC	• David's seven years of tribulation (age 23-30)
1055 BC	• David anointed King of Judah at Hebron after Saul's death (age 30) — David conquers Jerusalem
1048 BC	• David anointed king over all Israel at Jerusalem (age 37) — In the immediate years following: David recovers the ark; the Lord's covenant is made with David; David achieves military victories
1035 BC	• David's grave sin against Uriah and Bathsheba (age 50) — David's numbering the people (date uncertain)
1034-1015 BC	• David's lavish preparations for the Temple (age 51-70)
1015 BC	• David's death (age 70); Solomon reigns as king

Part One

God Prepares David, His Chosen

Day One

Breaking Generational Curses

▶ Scripture Reading: Ruth 4:9-21

No...Moabite or any of his descendants may enter the assembly of the LORD,* even down to the tenth generation. ... Do not seek a treaty of friendship with them as long as you live.

Deuteronomy 23:3,6

How sobering to find out that you were headed for destruction even before you were conceived! How crushing to realize that the sins of generations were heaped upon your shoulders even before you were born! So it was with David. David's family tree, sketched out for us at the end of the Book of Ruth, places David only three generations from Ruth the Moabitess. Ruth, the foreigner from Moab, had married Boaz the Bethlehemite. The son born to them was Obed; whose son, in turn, was Jesse; whose son, in turn, was David (see Ruth 4:21-22). The generational curse stemming from Ruth's forefather, recorded in Deuteronomy, hung over David's head: "No...Moabite or any of his

descendants may enter the assembly of the LORD. ... Do
not seek a treaty of friendship with them as long as you
live." The Moabites failed to aid the Israelites on their
journey from Egypt. Instead they hired Balaam to pronounce a curse against Israel, which God miraculously
turned into a blessing. But then God, in turn, judged the
Moabites and all their descendants by excluding them from
His presence and from the friendship of His house down to
the tenth generation!

I remember, early in my own Christian experience,
pondering an observation a Christian author made that all
truly great men and women of God were invariably second-
or third-generation Christians. Their greatness could be
traced to their spiritual inheritance and to their godly,
prayerful upbringing that breathed the very fire of God into
their souls. I remember the pain that filled my own heart as
I realized that I was the *first* member of my whole family to
come to Christ and that my ancestors—with alcoholics on
both sides of the line—had marked and stained our family
tree with what Peter called that "empty [futile] way of life
handed down to you from your forefathers" (1 Pet. 1:18).
I felt myself under a generational curse similar to David's.

I am so glad Peter reminds us that "it was not with
perishable things such as silver or gold that you were
*redeemed from the empty way of life handed down to you
from your forefathers,* but with the precious blood of Christ,
a lamb without blemish or defect. ... chosen before the
creation of the world..." (1 Pet. 1:18-19).

And so, by touching the delivering mercy and redeeming grace of God, David witnessed that generational curse broken in his own life. In an awesome way he was enabled to enter the presence of the Lord and the rich friendship of his God. I am sure that Ruth also helped pave the way for her great-grandson David, as she herself pressed into "the LORD, the God of Israel, under whose wings [she had] come to take refuge" (Ruth 2:12).

Jesus declares in Revelation 22:16, "I am the Root...of David." In the world of horticulture inferior stock is used to receive the grafts of good branches, and so good fruit is born. In the amazing science of God, however, otherwise useless and wild branches are grafted—contrary to nature—into a new and holy root system. Consequently glorious fruit is borne by the miracle-working power of God! (See Romans 11:17,24.) Jehovah had indeed grafted David into a new "root system." In himself, David was a useless branch, growing from a cursed Moabite root. But by Jehovah's grace, David was grafted into our Lord Jesus Christ. Jesus became the Root of David. By grace David now had the finest of genealogies! This same grace, I saw, was available to me! I did not have to live in the shadow of a stained ancestry. I did not have to live under the curse of generations of alcoholism. Jesus, by the power of His precious blood, severed me from my ancestral past and rooted me deep in Himself: God's "Lamb *without blemish or defect*." What a perfect heritage! He is now my brand-new ancestry! He is now my holy genealogy! Now I can press on—uninhibited—into the presence of my God and into the friendship of my Lord!

Come, hear David's own words of faith:

> Unto You, O LORD, do I bring my life. ...
> Remember, O LORD, Your tender mercies and
> loving-kindnesses; for they have been ever of old.
> Remember not [my lapses and frailties] the sins of
> my youth, nor my transgressions; according to
> Your mercy and steadfast love remember me for
> Your goodness' sake, O LORD. ... For Your name's
> sake, O LORD, pardon my iniquity and my guilt,
> for they are great. ... The secret [of the sweet,
> satisfying companionship] of the LORD have they
> who fear—revere and worship—Him, and He will
> show them His covenant, and reveal to them its
> [deep, inner] meaning (Psalm 25:1,6-7,11,14 AMP).

Taking a Step of Faith

*My Father, You know me through and through.
Nothing about me is hidden from Your sight. You know the
woof and the warp of my complex being. You see my own
personal sin and guilt, and You see every strand from my
perverse ancestry as it was woven into the fabric of my
being. I now come to You in faith to claim the redeeming
work of Your dear Son.*

*Lord Jesus, I take Your all-powerful blood as the
cleansing for all my own personal defilement and sin. I
receive Your forgiveness and Your cleansing. I take Your
precious blood, spotless Lamb of God, as the divine laser*

that severs me from my fallen root system, redeeming me "from the empty way of life handed down...from [my] forefathers." I declare, in faith, that every generational curse is broken in my life!

Blessed Holy Spirit, I receive Your engrafting work! I believe You have grafted me into Jesus, the Root of David. I take, by faith, my place in my new genealogy, in my brand new ancestry, and in my holy heritage!

*I thank You, thrice-holy Lord, that I am a brand-new creation! The old **has** passed away. All things **have** become new! Thank You, in Jesus' name; thank You! Amen.*

---

*Where the word form "LORD" appears in the Scripture text, the four holy consonants *YHVH* (the tetragram) are being translated. These four letters are pronounced either as **Jehovah** or **Yahweh**, depending on the vowel sounds used. This is the grand covenant name of the God of Israel, the name David delighted to call upon.

Day Two

An Illegitimate Son

▶ Scripture Reading: Psalm 89:15-37

> *Surely I was sinful at birth, sinful from the time my mother conceived me.*
>
> *Psalm 51:5*

Theologians quote these statements from David's confession in Psalm 51 to support the doctrine of total depravity from birth. I am sure this is a reasonable use of this Scripture. However, I do not want to overlook another very important, possible implication in these statements.

David's life story is told for us in First and Second Samuel, the first two chapters of First Kings, and the Book of First Chronicles. The first mention of David by name in this whole narrative is in First Samuel, chapter 16. This chapter tells the story of Samuel's arrival at the house of Jesse in Bethlehem under a divine commission to anoint the future king of Israel. We are told that Samuel, in obedience, "consecrated Jesse and his sons and invited them to the sacrifice." At the appointed place, Samuel looked over all seven of Jesse's sons: Eliab, Abinadab, Shammah, Shimea, Nethanel, Raddai, and Ozem. Though all were very promising, to none of them did the Spirit bear witness that this was Israel's anointed future king. Finally, a perplexed Samuel concluded, "The LORD has not chosen these." Then he asked Jesse, "Are these all the sons you have?" Jesse's response is interesting: "There is still the youngest, but he is *tending the sheep*." I have asked myself, *Why was David not included in this most important event?* Tending the sheep was not a sufficient reason in itself to be excluded from this most important event; when Jesse needed David to take supplies down to his three older brothers, soldiers in the Valley of Elah, David dutifully went, having "left the flock *with a keeper*" (1 Sam. 17:20 NASB). Could there be another reason David was not included? Was Jesse perhaps embarrassed over his teenage son David? Just what, exactly, did David mean when he said that he was "shapen in iniquity" and conceived in sin (Ps. 51: 5 KJV)? Why did David grieve over his parents' rejection of him in Psalm 27:10 (NASB), "my father and my mother have forsaken me"? Why was he "estranged from [his] brothers, and an alien to [his] mother's sons" (Ps. 69:8 NASB)? Why did Eliab, his oldest brother, treat him with such contempt at Elah: "...I know how conceited you are and how wicked your heart is..." (1 Sam. 17:28)? Is there something in all these statements that holds a key that would explain why David would grow up to be such an emotionally broken and inadequate man? I believe there is.

We tend, naturally, to follow in the ways of our past. Judah, the great ancestor of Jesse, ensnared his own feet in Genesis 38 when he went looking for a prostitute by the side of the road. What a shock, after one night of illicit pleasure, for Judah to find out the consequence. He had unknowingly gone to bed with Tamar, his own daughter-in-law! The report was brought to his ears, "Your daughter-in-law Tamar is guilty of prostitution, and as a result she is now pregnant" (Gen. 38:24). But out of this same moral blemish would grow the family tree of Judah. This was Jesse's heritage, and David's, and consequently, Jesus' (see Mt. 1:3).

These were Jesse's roots. Is it possible that David's conception was under a similar circumstance—that is, conceived in sin? I understand tradition holds out the possibility that David was Jesse's son, but the fruit of an indiscriminate act of passion with some unnamed woman. In this light, all the above Scriptures would make more sense, including Jesse's excluding David from Samuel's feast. In this light, I can understand more clearly something of David's emotional brokenness and the bitter roots contributing to David's personal dysfunction and his inadequacy as a husband and a father (a subject we will explore later). If this was indeed true, then I can understand how yet another millstone was hung around David's neck, for "No one born of a forbidden marriage [of illegitimate birth] nor any of his descendants may enter the assembly of the LORD, even down to the tenth generation" (Deut 23:2).

David did grieve over his parents' rejection for whatever reason, but in his anguish he found a further measure of the Lord's redeeming love. "...Do not abandon me nor forsake me, O God of my salvation! For my father and my mother have forsaken me, *but the LORD will take me up*" (Ps. 27:9-10 NASB).

One of the most powerfully redeeming revelations ever to come to David is recorded for us in Psalm 89, a psalm of Ethan, who was one of "the men David put in charge of the music in the house of the LORD" (1 Chronicles 6:31,44). In his brilliant song, Ethan recounted an awesome revelation:

> Once you spoke in a vision, to your faithful people you said...I have found David my servant; with my sacred oil I have anointed him. ... My faithful love will be with him. ... He will call out to me, 'You are my Father. ...' I will also appoint him my first-born. ... I will maintain my love to him forever, and my covenant with him will never fail. I will establish his line forever, his throne as long as the heavens endure (Psalm 89:19-29).

Jehovah had taken David to be His firstborn son! The Lord *Himself* became David's father!

Perhaps for this redeeming reason and in this healing light David, in Psalm 139, was able to draw Jehovah back, by faith, to that fateful night of his conception and declare:

> For *you* created my inmost being; *you* knit me together in my mother's womb. *I praise you* because I am fearfully and wonderfully made; *your* works are wonderful, I know that full well. My frame was not hidden from *you* when I was made in the secret place. When I was woven together...*your* eyes saw my unformed body. ... How precious to me are *your* thoughts, O God! How vast is the sum of them! Were I to count

them, they would outnumber the grains of sand...
(Psalm 139:13-18).

How marvelous is the covenant love of our God, which
enables us to trade the rags of our polluted beginnings and
all our painful rejections for the riches of His unfailing
love. David may have lacked Jesse's love, but Jehovah
took David as His very own son, His firstborn son, and He
promised He would love him forever!

My own father was a good provider but a poor
nurturer. I never remember him visibly loving me, holding
me close to him, or hugging me. I am sure his alcoholic
parents never pressed him close to them either. He grew up
broken and his son grew up broken. But one day I was
introduced to a Father who would *always* love me and who
would *ever* care for me. In that steadfast love I have found
that we—you and I—can be healed and restored and made
whole!

Taking a Step of Faith

*Father, You know the pain of my past. You know what
I lack; You know my needs. But I thank You that You have
adopted me as **Your** very own child through Jesus Christ!
I thank **You** for **Your** steadfast love that will never fail me.
I thank You that You will never leave me, never abandon
me, and never forsake me. I receive from You Your healing
love. I believe You will rebuild all the broken places in my
life for Jesus' sake! Amen.*

Day Three

God Was Looking for David

▶ Scripture Reading: 1 Samuel 16:1-13

I have found David my servant; with my sacred oil
I have anointed him.

Psalm 89:20

God was apparently looking for David. At least that
thought seems inherent in the words, "I have *found* David
...." It is believed by some chronologers that David was not
yet born when Samuel declared to the apostate Saul:
"...The LORD has sought out for Himself a man after His
own heart, and the LORD has appointed him as ruler over
His people, because you have not kept what the LORD
commanded you" (1 Sam. 13:14 NASB). So God was
searching, in His awesome foreknowledge and in His
sovereign choosings, for a man with a heart like His own.
Paul, in Acts 13:22 (NASB) added God's own thought
about David being a man after His own heart—one "*who*
will do all My will." Later in this very same account, Paul
summarizes David's life in these words: "...he had served

the purpose of God in his own generation..." (Acts 13:36 NASB). David was a man with a zealous heart toward God and a passionate zeal to do the will of God.

Jehovah is still searching for souls like David—searching by His prescience from eternity and by His omniscience in time. "For the eyes of the LORD run to and fro throughout the whole earth, to show Himself strong in the behalf of them whose heart is perfect toward Him" (2 Chron. 16:9a KJV). To those with a passionate heart such as David's Jehovah comes in the anointing of His Holy Spirit to empower them to fulfill His purpose and will.

Charles Wesley, Methodism's troubadour, sings about this sacred anointing in his hymn, "Jesus, Thine All Victorious Love:"

> Jesus, Thine all victorious love
> Shed in my heart abroad;
> Then shall my feet no longer rove,
> Rooted and fixed in God.
>
> O that in me the sacred fire
> Might now begin to glow;
> Burn up the dross of base desire,
> And make the mountains flow!
>
> Refining fire, go through my heart;
> Illuminate my soul;
> Scatter Thy life through every part,
> And sanctify the whole.
>
> My steadfast soul, from falling free,
> Shall then no longer rove,
> While Christ is all the world to me,
> And all my heart is love.

It is into this holy anointing that David, probably still in his teens, was brought by the hand of Samuel the prophet. In the midst of Jesse and his sons on that hallowed day, "...Samuel took the horn of oil and anointed him in the presence of his brothers, and *from that day on the Spirit of the LORD came upon David in power*" (1 Sam. 16:13). At the end of his life, more than 50 years later, David would bear witness that he was yet "the man anointed by the God of Jacob" and that "the Spirit of the LORD spoke through me; His word was on my tongue" (2 Sam. 23:1-2). Even in his darkest hour of sinful defeat, David cried out for this above all else: "Do not cast me from Your presence *or take Your Holy Spirit from me*" (Ps. 51:11).

The whole of David's life can be understood only in the light of the continued anointing of the Holy Spirit upon him. That anointing had taken his natural, musical skills (1 Sam. 16:17-18) and transformed them into a prophetic gift of the Holy Spirit. David was "the man anointed by the God of Jacob" as "Israel's singer of songs" (2 Sam. 23:1). Half of the songs in our Book of Psalms bears David's name. A number of them are prophetic and messianic in content. Peter, in Acts 2:30-31, identified David as *a prophet* who in his songs foresaw the coming of our Lord Jesus Christ. David was an anointed man. His secret in service was the power of the Spirit of God; the gains in his own personal life were by the indwelling presence of the Holy Spirit; and what he deeply feared the most was the loss of that anointing by his compromise with sin.

The final word of Jesus to His followers before He ascended to His Father in Heaven was that they should not leave Jerusalem until they had been "clothed with power from on high" (Lk. 24:49). He enjoined them: "...wait for the gift My Father promised. ... But you *will* receive power when the Holy Spirit comes on you; and you *will* be My witnesses..." (Acts 1:4,8). That same "promise is...*for all* whom the Lord our God will call" (Acts 2:39).

I remember the night in May of 1953 when, as a youth of 16, I knelt beside my bed in my parents' Brooklyn, New York, apartment and believed that *this* promise was for *me*. I claimed the inspired words of John: "This is the confidence we have in approaching God: that if we ask anything according to His will, He hears us. And if we know that He hears us—whatever we ask—*we know that we have* what we asked of Him" (1 Jn. 5:14-15). That very night I was filled with the Holy Spirit, and my life seemed to me to be more revolutionized than when I first came to Christ several years before! What Jesus had promised was true. I received power when the Holy Spirit came upon me—and I would be His witness.

Taking a Step of Faith

Lord Jesus, You have promised "how much more will your Father in heaven give the Holy Spirit to those who ask Him!" I come boldly before the throne of God to ask.

*Father, I ask You to fill me to overflowing with the Holy Spirit and with power. Because I know I am asking according to Your will, I know You hear me. And because I know You hear me, I thank You that **I now have what I have asked of You!** I receive from Your hand the fullness of Your blessed Spirit! Thank You, Father, for I ask this in Jesus' precious name. Amen.*

Day Four

The Bigger They Are,
The Harder They Fall

▶ Scripture Reading: 1 Samuel 17

A champion named Goliath, who was from Gath, came out of the Philistine camp. He was over nine feet tall.

1 Samuel 17:4

Fifteen miles west of Bethlehem you will find, even to this day, the gently sloping Valley of Elah. It was here that the armies of Saul had one of their confrontations with the armies of the Philistines. Out of this Philistine camp strode their champion, Goliath, a giant from the city of Gath. We learn from Joshua 11:22 that in the days of the conquest of Canaan there were Anakim living in the Philistine cities of Gaza, Gath, and Ashdod. The Anakim are represented on Egyptian monuments as a tall and fair people. These were undoubtedly the "giants in the land" who had originally terrified the ten spies in Numbers and overwhelmed them with unbelief. Now a champion from among them stood to defy the ranks of Israel. That giants exist in the earth is not fantasy. I recently read of a man from Bangladesh who is 8 feet 3 inches tall, and of a 7-foot, 6-inch-tall Pakistani. Goliath himself was a full 9 feet tall. He carried 150 pounds of bronze armor on his massive body, and in his hand was a long spear with a bronze spearhead weighing a good 15 pounds. Standing in the midst of the Valley of Elah, a perfect echo chamber, he shouted defiance and curses and taunts against Israel and Israel's Keeper.

Formidable foes are always threatening our lives; spiritual giants of passion, pride, anxiety, and fear are powerfully arrayed against us. They are deployed to keep us from our spiritual inheritance in Christ. It is wise for us, therefore, to study the faith responses of David Ben Jesse to his foe and then to translate these holy responses into our own experiences so we too might become "more than conquerors through Him who loved us" (Rom. 8:37).

Sent by Jesse to take a needed care package down to his three older brothers serving in Saul's armies, David, Jesse's youngest son, arrived at the Valley of Elah on this particular day just in time to hear "this uncircumcised Philistine...defy the armies of the living God" (1 Sam. 16:26). David determined to resist him!

But there were obstacles to discourage that leap of faith David would make. Eliab, his oldest brother, poured withering scorn and chilling invective on David's heart of faith: "...I know how conceited you are and how wicked your heart is..." (1 Sam. 16:28). Saul's crippling words of unbelief, as yet another fiery dart, struck at David's heart: *"You are not able..."* (1 Sam. 16:33). Then there was Goliath's scorn of David: "...he despised him... He said to David, 'Am I a dog, that you come at me with sticks?'" (1 Sam. 16:42-43)

In answer to this barrage of discouragement, the stripling David began to confess a dynamic trust and faith in the power of the living God. Speaking of Jehovah who had delivered him in the past from a 300-pound lion and a 600-pound bear, David confessed these powerful faith words: *"Jehovah will deliver me!"* (see 1 Sam. 17:37) His undaunted confession of faith flew in the face of the unbelief of all who surrounded him. *"Jehovah will deliver me!"*

David then spoke that same word of faith into the face of the powers of darkness. *Young's Concordance* tells us that "Goliath" may mean "soothsayer." Undoubtedly Goliath *was* in tune with the world of evil spirits and sorcery. Perhaps for that reason David refused to empower him by even once calling him "Goliath," but referred to him only as "this uncircumcised [outside of the covenant] Philistine." This was David's confession of faith in the face of the giant:

> I come against you in the name of the LORD Almighty [Jehovah of Hosts], the God of the armies of Israel.... This day the LORD *will* hand you over to me, and I *will* strike you down and cut off your head. Today I *will* give the carcasses of the

Philistine army to the birds of the air and the
beasts of the earth, and *the whole world will know
that there is a God in Israel.* ...the battle is the
LORD's, and He *will* give all of you into our hands
(1 Samuel 17:45-47).

What a powerful confession of faith! David had his eye on
Jehovah of Hosts, the God of all the armies of Heaven, and
they would fight—in spiritual warfare—on David's behalf!

Did you ever wonder what went through David's mind
as he stepped onto that valley floor and began to walk
toward Goliath with a little stick in one hand, five smooth
stones in his shepherd's bag, and a sling in his other hand?
(By the way, David took *five* smooth stones not because he
doubted he would succeed in killing Goliath at the very
first shot, but because, according to Second Samuel 21:22,
there were four more giants around like Goliath, and David
was preparing for them too. He was a man in pursuit of a
total victory that day!)

I believe that as David stepped out on the valley floor,
he was singing the words of what would become our Psalm
8, "a psalm of David," a song referring to the Philistine city
of Gath (*gittith*). David sang: "O LORD, our LORD, how
majestic is Your name in all the earth... You have ordained
praise because of Your enemies, to silence the foe and the
avenger" (Ps. 8:1-2). Then, with an eye of faith, seeing
himself as Jehovah saw him, David cried out, "What
is...the son of man that you care for him? You...crowned
him with glory and honor. You made him *ruler* over the

works of Your hands; *You put everything under his feet....*
O LORD, our LORD, how majestic is Your name in all the
earth!" (Ps. 8:4-9). The rest is history.

> David ran quickly toward the battle line to meet
> him. Reaching into his bag and taking out a stone,
> he slung it and struck the Philistine on the
> forehead. The stone sank into his forehead, and he
> fell facedown on the ground. So David triumphed
> over the Philistine with a sling and a stone; with-
> out a sword in his hand he struck down the Philis-
> tine and killed him (1 Samuel 17:48-50).

David then beheaded Goliath with the giant's own
sword. In the mass confusion that followed, the Philistines
turned and ran, pursued by the armies of Israel and Judah
to the very entrance of Gath and the very gates of Ekron,
their Philistine dead lying all along the highway.

David then took the giant's rotting skull, we are told,
brought it to the city of Jerusalem (1 Sam. 17:54), and
entombed it in a place that, I believe, would thereafter be
known as "the Place of the Skull"—*Golgotha* in Hebrew;
Calvary in Latin.

What lessons may we take for ourselves from this
faith-building account? Surely, that One has come, the
greater Son of David, not with five smooth stones but with
five bleeding wounds, to defeat fully and forever, once and
for all, our mortal enemy: our Goliath. The sign of that
victory remains to this day at the Place of the Skull, at
Golgotha, at Calvary! (see Matthew 27:33)

Because of *that* great and comprehensive victory, we can stand tall in the awesome truth that "everyone born of God overcomes the world. This is the victory that has overcome the world, even our faith. Who is it that overcomes the world? Only he who *believes that Jesus is the Son of God*" (1 Jn. 5:4-5).

Taking a Step of Faith

Father, You see the Goliaths who fiercely oppose me: giants of unbelief, fear, worry, lust, lack of self-control, anger, and depression. I come to You to receive Your overcoming grace and Your strength!

Lord Jesus, I see Your finished work for me. I see You, by Your death, destroying him who holds the power of death; that is, the devil. I see You freeing me from my slavery to fear; I see You powerfully helping me in the hours of my greatest temptations!

Spirit of the living God, I see You anointing my lips with a positive confession of faith. Forgive my words of unbelief. Purge me from confessions of fear, self-pity, and doubt. Fill my mouth with David's own words of faith!

*Most Holy God, I **do** believe the bigger they are, the harder they fall! And I take my place in Jesus' triumph this day, in His all-victorious name! Amen.*

Day Five

Friendships That Heal and Restore

▶ Scripture Reading: 1 Samuel 18:1-4 and
1 Samuel 20

Jonathan, Saul's son, greatly delighted in David.
1 Samuel 19:1 KJV

We all are in need of friendship. Everyone needs at least one good friend. God has given us friendships as relationships that can heal and restore. A true friend can bring out God's best in our lives. I find myself so thankful to the Lord for those healing, restoring relationships in my own life down through the years, for every *true* friend He has given to me.

I carry an anonymous quote in the front of my Bible which reads:

What is a friend? Friends are people with whom you can dare to be yourself. Your soul can be open with them. They ask you to put on nothing, only to be what you are. When you are with them you do not have to be on your guard. You can say what you think, as long as it is genuinely you. Friends understand those contradictions in your nature that lead others to misjudge you. With them you can breathe freely. They understand. You can keep still with them. It makes no matter. They are like fire that purges to the bone. You can weep with them, sing with them, laugh with them, pray with them. Through it all they see, know, and love you. What is a friend? Just one, I repeat, with whom you can dare to be yourself.

Jonathan, the son of Saul, was a friend to David. At this juncture in our narrative (1 Samuel 18), the Holy Spirit allows us, for one brief sacred moment of time, to look into the depths of the hearts of these two men and see the divine creation of a friendship—which seems far more awesome, I think, than the creation of a world. It is a relationship that will help bring healing and restoration to those wounded and chaotic places in the heart of David.

We may tend to think of David and Jonathan as two young schoolboys hanging out together in the fields of Bethlehem. In actuality, David was probably over 20 years old at this point, and Prince Jonathan was about 40 years of age. Forsaken by his parents and estranged from his brothers (see Psalm 27:10; 69:8), David found in Jonathan a father and a brother—a friend who would love him all his life through. F.B. Meyer, in his book, *David: Shepherd,*

Psalmist, King, comments on this very thought: David "had lost Eliab [see First Samuel 17:28] in the morning; but at nightfall he had won a friend that would stick closer than a brother."[1]

Just after the overwhelming defeat of Goliath, David was brought before King Saul.

> Now it came about when [David] had finished speaking to Saul, that the soul of Jonathan was knit to the soul of David, and Jonathan loved him as himself. ... Then Jonathan made a covenant with David because he loved him as himself. And Jonathan stripped himself of the robe that was on him and gave it to David, with his armor, including his sword and his bow and his belt (1 Samuel 18:1,3-4 NASB).

So the soul of Jonathan was *divinely knit* to the soul of David. The LORD did between them what He desires to do between all the members of His Body—make them "of one heart and soul" (Acts 4:32 NASB). Matthew Henry comments about David and Jonathan that one soul lived in two bodies. They were divinely knit as "one new man"—a prototype of the Body of Christ.

Jonathan introduced David to the holy concept of *covenant*; "Jonathan made a covenant with David because he loved him as himself." This covenant would be affirmed again (1 Sam. 20:17) and again (1 Sam. 20:42) and again (1 Sam. 23:18). In their covenant, these two men tasted the powers of the new covenant to come; the very expression "because he loved him as himself" became new covenant language on the lips of our Lord Jesus (see Mt. 22:35-40).

The great seal and insignia of God's ancient people, Israel, is the Star of David. Thoughts of its origins are varied, for it appears as a pagan symbol as early as the Bronze Age, the Age of the Patriarchs (3,000-4,000 BC). I personally believe that Israel's adoption of the Star of David is related to David's revelation of covenant, as David himself became a covenant-hearted man. David continually celebrated Jehovah's covenant love (*hesed*, in Hebrew), and he speaks repeatedly in his psalms about Jehovah's covenant. Among his brethren, David is also a covenant maker and a covenant keeper: "So all the elders of Israel came to the king at Hebron, and King David *made a covenant with them* before the LORD at Hebron..." (2 Sam. 5:3; see also 1 Chron. 11:3 NASB). The Star of David, made from joining two equilateral triangles, celebrates the union of a man—spirit, soul, and body—with his God—Father, Son, and Holy Spirit. It also celebrates the holy union of a man with his wife, of a father with his son, of a brother with his brother, and of a sister with her sister—the joining of heart to heart in the holy love of God.

Because of their covenant relationship, Jonathan stripped himself of his robe, his armor, his sword, his bow, and his belt—even his very throne—and gave them all away to David. When David wore Jonathan's kingly robe, one could easily mistake David for Jonathan at first glance. In the royal court, David became Jonathan's *alter ego*, his other self. In all this, Jonathan was actually releasing David from being the rejected, abandoned boy and helping David become the man of God, David the King! This was a relationship divinely intended to heal and restore.

Again and again in the seven ensuing years of misunderstanding and devastation, Jonathan would stand by David's side as his friend and as his protector. In reality, the only true friends we ever have are those who are still our friends after a time of misunderstanding and devastation. Jonathan was that kind of a friend to David. The very faith-filled, prophetic words of Psalm 63 (which we will comment on in a later chapter) were framed by David after his final time together with Jonathan in the wilderness of Ziph (see 1 Sam. 23:15-18). Seven years later when Jonathan—slain by the Philistines—lay dead on the mountains of Gilboa, the agonizing cry that arose from David's lips in Second Samuel 1 reveals to us even more of the holy depths of their friendship. The loss of Jonathan in David's life was a seemingly incalculable loss. Jonathan, as his name declares, was Jehovah's *gift* to David, but now David would be pressed into finding a deeper love relationship with the Giver Himself. All through his life David would always want someone to be at his side, such as Hushai the Arkite, a part of his royal cabinet, whose only reason for being there was simply that he was "the king's friend" (see 1 Chron. 27:33). Jonathan had left his mark upon David's soul. He had planted a seed in David's heart that would continue to grow and bear fruit to the very end of his life.

Well may we thank God for those friendships He has given us that heal and restore: preeminently friendship with Himself; then the friendship of a husband with his wife, of a father with his child, and of one brother or sister in the Body of Christ with yet another—all joined and knit by the Spirit of God.

The redemptive purpose and the very core value in all friendships is *integrity*. Integrity is defined as "the quality or state of being complete, unbroken, whole, entire, unimpaired, sound, upright, honest, sincere." This is the essence and the goal of all godly friendships.

Alan Redpath, in his book, *The Making of a Man of God*, celebrates God's answer to our human need:

> ...it is God's plan for souls to be knit together.... The human heart has cried out that it might be knit to another as Jonathan was knit to David.... Therefore every true friendship, every real Christian courtship, every genuine oneness in marriage, is a re-establishment of this sacred union; it was God's purpose from before the foundation of the world.[2]

Taking a Step of Faith

*Lord Jesus, You are my dearest friend and my fondest brother. Heavenly Father, You are "my great Father, and I thy true son." By the power of Your Holy Spirit I receive Your healing friendship, and I enter into Your restoring love! I also thank You for every human vessel and for every earthly channel of Your healing covenant love to me. Grant me the grace to see **You** always as the source and to hold You, Lord, as preeminent in my heart above anyone else through whom You may choose to love me. In turn, make me a channel through which Your healing, restoring love can flow into the needy hearts of those to whom You have joined me. I believe for this in the name of Jesus. Amen.*

Day Six

Seven Years of
Personal Tribulation

▶ Scripture Reading: 1 Samuel 18:5-30

And Saul sought him [David] every day, but God did not deliver him into his hand.
                                        1 Samuel 23:14 NASB

After the defeat of Goliath and the routing of the armies of the Philistines, the popularity of David inspired a song in the land of Israel: "Saul has slain his thousands, and David his tens of thousands" (1 Sam. 18:7). Women danced in the streets to the new tune. But we are told that "Saul was very angry; this refrain galled him..." (1 Sam. 18:8). David had captured the hearts of Saul's son, Jonathan, who became David's best friend, and of Saul's daughter, Michal, who then became David's wife. Now the hearts of all Israel were in love with David, and Saul was insanely jealous of him. In his jealousy, Saul sought repeatedly to kill young David. Initially, he tried to spear

him to the palace wall. Saul further stalked David at his
own home in order to put him to death. Finally, Saul
hunted David for what would be David's seven years of
personal tribulation in the wilderness of Judah, driving him
away as an exile among the Philistines.

I think of the tragic losses in David's life during these
seven long, dark years. As a young man in his twenties,
David suffered the loss of his hero, Saul. I am sure many
were the nights that David cried himself to sleep, trying to
understand why this man, for whose honor he had jeopar-
dized his life, had now become his inveterate enemy.
David likewise suffered the loss of his young wife, Michal,
for in a pitiless act of vengeance, Saul gave Michal to
another man. Finally, David suffered the great loss of his
dearest friend, Jonathan, on the mountains of Gilboa. These
were the darkest years in the life of this young man of God.

A man with a lesser passion for God could have
become embittered and overthrown by these reverses, but
David emerged from his seven years of tribulation better
not bitter. The words of Psalm 18 (recorded again for us
in Second Samuel 22) reveal the vast treasures David
uncovered in his darkness.

> David sang to the LORD the words of this song
> when the LORD delivered him from the hand of all
> his enemies and from the hand of Saul. He said:
> "[I love You, O LORD, my strength (Ps. 18:1)].
> The LORD is my rock, my fortress and my
> deliverer; my God is my rock, in whom I take
> refuge, my shield and the horn of my salvation.

He is my stronghold, my refuge and my
savior—from violent men you save me" (2 Samuel
22:1-3).

What treasure had David found in the darkness? It was the
treasure of fresh revelations of His God! David praised
God: "He brought me out into a spacious place" (2 Sam.
22:20). That broad place was none other than God Himself! The deeper knowledge of the Holy One had become
his rich find.

In asking ourselves *why* God allowed such losses in the
life of young David, we come up with only one possible
answer. The Lord invariably does not *cause* severe losses
in our lives—the death of a loved one, the loss of a wife, the
cruel rejections of our brethren—for it is "the *thief* [who]
comes only to steal and kill and destroy..." (Jn. 10:10).
Satan is the destroyer, the *cause* of our losses; however, the
Lord is sovereignly able to *use* our losses to draw us into
a deeper relationship with Himself. Perhaps, and especially
so in David's case, Jehovah would ensure a better future for
young David than for Saul. Saul initially seemed to make
the perfect king—humble, anointed, considerate, and selfless—but he was untried, unproven, and unbroken. Thus he
crashed and burned. He died as an enemy of God. It
would be different with David. The cruel dance of circumstances would be used by Jehovah to break him, melt him,
and mold him to become a man after Jehovah's own heart.
The following anonymous poem, which I have come to
appreciate more and more deeply over the years, sums up
David's experiences so well.

Pressed out of measure and
    pressed to all length;
Pressed so intensely, it seems
    beyond strength;
Pressed in the body, and
    pressed in the soul;
Pressed in the mind, till the
    dark surges roll.
Pressure by foes, and pressure
    by friends—
Pressure on pressure till life
    nearly ends.

Pressed into knowing no
    helper but God;
Pressed into loving the staff
    and the rod.
Pressed into liberty where
    nothing clings;
Pressed into faith for
    impossible things.
Pressed into tasting the joy of
    the Lord;
Pressed into living a Christlife
    outpoured!

Psalm 118 is anonymous in our Bibles, though it appears to be ascribed by Ezra to King David (cf. Psalm 118: 1,29 with Ezra 3:10-11). The style is surely Davidic. In it the psalmist recounts how the Lord helped him in his distress.

From my distress I called upon the LORD; the LORD answered me and set me in a large place. The LORD is for me; I will not fear; what can man do to me?... You pushed me violently so that I was falling, but the LORD helped me. The LORD is my strength and song, and He has become my salvation. ... The stone which the builders rejected has become the chief corner stone. This is the LORD's doing; it is marvelous in our eyes (Psalm 118:5-6,13-14,22-23).

C. H. Spurgeon in his book, *The Treasury of David*, comments on these messianic verses:

The Lord frequently appears to save the heaviest blows for his best-beloved ones; if any one affliction be more painful than another, it falls to the lot of those whom He most distinguishes in His service. ... David had been rejected by those in authority, but God had placed him in a position of the highest honor and the greatest usefulness, making him the chief cornerstone....

Martin Luther said of this psalm, "This is *my* psalm, my chosen psalm." There was a day when I too said of this psalm, "This is *my* psalm, my *very own* psalm." We are caused, at times, to go through deep valleys of grief and great crises of pain and sorrow; rejection and abandonment become our lot. A choice then becomes ours. We must choose that this trial shall not make us bitter—not bitter against a God who could have prevented it all and not bitter against that loved one or against those brothers who should

have known better, but who instead inflicted such deep pain
on us. We must rather choose that this circumstance will
make us better—better in knowing the faithfulness of a
delivering God, who always brings us out into "a large
place," and better in being more perfectly fitted to serve
Him in that enlarged place. Every morning I am now able
to rise with a deep thankfulness in my heart, for "the Lord
answered me and set me in a large place."

Taking a Step of Faith

*Father, You know the pain of my circumstances. I dare
not say You **caused** them, and surely You could have
prevented them, but now I know You will **use** them in my
life. I choose this day to receive Your dealings in my life.
I choose to believe "that in **all things** God works for the
good of those who love Him, who have been called according to His purpose." Press me close to Your heart, reveal
Yourself to me in new and wonderful ways, and groom me
for whatever "large place" of service You are calling me
into. By Your grace I will emerge from this time of great
tribulation better and not bitter! In Jesus' dear name.
Amen.*

Day Seven

A Total Contradiction

▶ Scripture Reading: 1 Samuel 21:1-9; 22:6-23

*I trust in God's unfailing love [*hesed*: covenant love] for ever and ever.*

Psalm 52:8

At this juncture in our narrative, Saul has unsuccessful-ly tried to kill young David twice by spearing him to the palace wall (2 Sam. 18:11; 19:10). In further rage, "Saul sent men to David's house to watch it and to *kill him in the morning*..." (1 Sam. 19:11). But David, with the help of his young wife Michal, escaped that night to the prophet Samuel at Ramah, about ten miles north of Jerusalem. This would be the start of a series of miraculous interventions by God in delivering young David from the insane rages of Saul. The writing of Psalm 59 is attributed to David at this point in his life—"when Saul had sent men to watch David's house in order to kill him." Saul's determination that fateful night was to have David dead by morning, but David called upon the delivering power of God: "...save

49

me from bloodthirsty men. See how they lie in wait for me!... But I will sing of Your strength, *in the morning I will sing of Your love* [hesed: covenant love]; for You are my fortress, my refuge in times of trouble. O my Strength, I sing praise to You..." (Ps. 59:2-3,16-17). Thus the first rays of morning light found David very much alive, singing of the covenant love of Jehovah—his fortress, his refuge, and his strength!

With Saul on the march to Ramah, David went to seek out his dear friend Jonathan, who from this point on continued to interpose himself again and again between his father's hatred and the life of his young covenant-brother, David. It is important for us to note, however, especially in view of what is about to happen, that David's faith in Jehovah's keeping power, so eloquently expressed through-out Psalm 59, began to waver. David laid a snare for himself with the words of his own mouth as he expressed his fearful concern to Jonathan that "there is only a step between me and death" (1 Sam. 20:3). David, in view of his overwhelming circumstances, began to lose sight of Jehovah as his impenetrable fortress and as his secure refuge in times of trouble. His faith began to crumble.

David, fearing Saul's pursuit, then fled to Nob, a small town northeast of Jerusalem. There Ahimelech the high priest lived in a community with 85 other priests serving the tabernacle of God. David went to Nob to seek for provisions and for weapons (see 1 Sam. 21:3,8) and for a word from the Lord through Ahimelech the high priest. It is here that David experienced an abysmal and fearful collapse of his faith that released fatal consequences upon a whole community of innocent people. When pointedly questioned by Ahimelech about his secretive mission, David lied to the man of God: "The king charged me with a certain matter and said to me, 'No one is to know anything about your mission and your instructions'" (1 Sam. 21:2). Deceived by David, Ahimelech gave him the sacred bread of the Presence from the holy place for provisions, and for weaponry the sword of Goliath the Philistine that was wrapped in a cloth behind the ephod. (With these David, now even more irrationally crippled by fear, fled to Gath of all places; it was chief among the cities of the Philistines and the birthplace of Goliath!)

Perhaps it only partially dawned on David that day at Nob that "one of Saul's servants was there that day, *detained before the LORD*; he was Doeg the Edomite, Saul's head shepherd" (1 Sam. 21:7). This Doeg reported back to Saul the details of that fateful day: Ahimelech's giving David the holy bread, Goliath's sword, and words of guidance from Jehovah. On hearing this report Saul went and, by the willing hands of Doeg the Edomite, slaughtered Ahimelech and the whole priestly community for treason—including all the men, their wives, their children and babies, and their livestock! Only one man escaped, Ahimelech's son Abiathar, who then related to David the horror of that grisly slaughter.

On hearing the report, David, in deep anguish, cried out, "I am responsible for the death of your father's whole family" (1 Sam. 22:22b). The blood of hundreds of innocent people covered the hands of young David that day! His deceit had destroyed a whole village.

Alan Redpath in his book, *The Making of a Man of God*, comments on this grievous event: "...there sometimes come moments when darkness seems to fall, the sun seems to set, and to the man himself everything seems lost. Other people, observing his life, wonder if he is sinking beyond all hope of recovery."[3]   The lyrics of David's Psalm 52 come down to us through the centuries in review of this disaster; they record David's anguished thoughts when he realized that "Doeg the Edomite had gone to Saul and told him: 'David has gone to the house of Ahimelech.'"   The prophetic curse David pronounced on Doeg in this psalm was justified: "You...are a disgrace in the eyes of God... Surely God will bring you down to everlasting ruin: He will snatch you up and tear you from your tent; He will uproot you from the land of the living. ... Here now is the man who...grew strong by destroying others!" (Ps. 52:1,5,7)

Then, in contrast to this curse on Doeg, David cried out concerning himself, "But I am like an olive tree flourishing in the house of God; *I trust in God's unfailing love for ever and ever.* I will praise You forever for what You have done; in Your name I will hope, for Your name is good. I will praise You in the presence of Your saints" (Ps. 52:8-9).

Reading these words and contrasting them with David's fear-filled, lying, deceptive behavior, we are left confused. David's actions appeared as a total contradiction to his words. How could David "*trust* in God's unfailing [covenant] love for ever and ever," yet, in his cowardice and fear, have so deceived Ahimelech and caused the unwarranted death of a whole innocent community? I do not believe we have to go very far to find the answer. We need only look at our own lives. Have not we ourselves, at times, by our own speech and behavior, been a total contradiction to our own deepest inner commitments before God? Because these commitments do not lessen our responsibility for those sinful contradictions, we are compelled to fall, in deep repentance, at the feet of our God. In His mercy, God not only judges the sinfulness of our contradictions, but also sees the holy commitments of our heart. He sees and evaluates the hidden man of the heart. So, as we examine the contradictions in our own lives, we are better able to understand the contradictions in young David's life. Perhaps in touch with his own personal contradictions, Charles Wesley in his hymn, "Depth of Mercy," is compelled to ask:

> Depth of Mercy: can there be
> Mercy still reserved for me?
> Can my God his wrath forbear?
> Me, the chief of sinners spare?

> I have long withstood His grace,
> Long provoked Him to His face;
> Would not hearken to His calls,
> Grieved Him by a thousand falls.

> Whence to me this waste of love.
> Ask my Advocate above!
> See the cause in Jesus' face,
> Now before the throne of grace.

There for me the Savior stands,
Shows His wounds, and spreads His hands:
God is love, I know, I feel:
Jesus lives and loves me still.

If I rightly read Thy heart,
If Thou all compassion art,
Bow Thine ear, in mercy bow,
Pardon and accept me now!

Thus we come, as did David and Wesley, to cast ourselves in faith upon the covenant love of our God for ever and ever!

Taking a Step of Faith

Father, I have not always acted according to my true self, my inner heart where Christ dwells. By my words and by my actions I have been a contradiction to my deepest consecrations before You. But I now come to You in deep repentance and in faith, believing that the blood of Your everlasting covenant will wash away the guilt of those sinful contradictions and that Your Spirit of grace will strengthen the godly commitments of my inner man, that I may be a living expression of what You have birthed within the deepest places of my heart! For Jesus' sake. Amen.

Day Eight

A Quantum Leap
From Fear to Faith

▶ Scripture Reading: 1 Samuel 21:10-15;
Psalms 34 and 56

*David...was **very much afraid** of Achish king of Gath.*

1 Samuel 21:12b

*I sought the LORD, and He answered me; **He delivered me from all my fears**.*

Psalm 34:4

Paul E. Billheimer tells us that:

Sometimes the only way God can work real brokenness in us is by our failure. The human spirit is so immense, so magnificent, so monumental, so rich in potential that without grace it aspires to be a god.... This is why God uses for His greatest purposes only meek people, people that have been broken, emptied of themselves,

55

delivered from their unholy ambitions to dethrone God.... Because the world worships success, sometimes the only way God can break us is by failure.... Strange as it may seem, apparent failure seems to be an instrument in God's hands in preparing His people for larger service.... If God is going to perfect Christlikeness in you and in me, it may sometimes involve the failure of our ambitions, of our plans, of our dreams, of our hopes.... *Failure is sometimes better than success.*

We are at a point in David's life where he is destined to be broken again and again on the wheel of failure. We can sense God is preparing him through these losses for the ultimate fulfillment of his calling. At the end of our last account we left David with the holy showbread and Goliath's sword in hand, fleeing "for fear of Saul." David had deceived Ahimelech the priest to get these earthy provisions, but in so doing had left Ahimelech guilty of charges of conspiracy against Saul and treason against the monarchy.

In his irrational fear, David made another, more irrational move. Hunted and hounded throughout the cities and towns of Judah, David fled for sanctuary within the Philistine borders. Carrying on his person the sword of Goliath, David requested refuge from King Achish, lord of the city of Gath—*the very city of Goliath*! But as the Philistine court servants began to reiterate to King Achish the maidens' song, which they sang after David had slain their Philistine champion Goliath, we are told that "David took these words *into his heart* and was *very much afraid* of Achish king of Gath" (1 Sam. 21:12).

Fear can be a crippling emotion. A wholesome fear is the reverential, worshipful fear of the Lord, but the fear of man inevitably brings a snare. The word *fear* is related to the word *fara*, meaning a "snare" or a "trap." There are *rational* fears—our God-given warning system—but there are also *irrational* fears, phobias, which are short circuits in that natural warning system. David was gripped by just such an irrational fear in the courts of Achish. As fear came in the door, faith flew out the window. Fear is defined as "a feeling of anxiety and agitation caused by the presence or nearness of danger, evil, pain. Fear is dread, terror, fright, apprehension." Fear can, and often does, precipitate panic and even depression.

Young David, knowing of no other escape, "feigned insanity in their presence; and while he was in their hands he acted like a madman, making marks [scribbling] on the doors of the gate and letting saliva run down his beard" (1 Sam. 21:13). Achish responded to this humiliating display with disdain: "Look at the man! He is insane! Why bring him to me? Am I so short of madmen that you have to bring this fellow here to carry on like this in front of me? Must this man come into my house?" (1 Sam. 21:14-15) With those words, Achish banished him from the city. So "David left Gath and escaped to the cave of Adullam" (1 Sam. 22:1a).

Many are the fears—even irrational fears—that seek to ensnare *us*. This has been true in my own life. We fear what men, what even our supposed brethren, can do to us; we fear rejection; we fear loss; we fear what the government will do to us; we fear the endtimes; we fear for our family's well-being; we fear financial upset; we fear sickness; we fear accidents; we fear death! We become anxious, frightened, agitated, and apprehensive! We panic and then fall into an abysmal pit of depression! We struggle over how we can ever make that quantum leap from fear to faith.

Two psalms come to us from the heart of David in these days of failure and humiliation. Psalm 34 and Psalm 56 contain David's secret to his leap of faith. Psalm 34 bears this title: "Of David. When he pretended to be insane before Abimelech, who drove him away, and he left." *Abimelech* (literally, *Aba-Melech*) was a formal title given to King Achish, which meant "Father-King." Other Near Eastern monarchs, such as the pharaohs of Egypt, took titles apart from their own given names. For example, *pharaoh* is believed to mean "Sun of the Great House." Psalm 56 carries another title: "For the director of music. To the tune of '*A Dove on Distant Oaks*.' Of David. A *miktam*. When the Philistines had seized him in Gath."

In both these psalms David pinpoints his difficulty: his fear of man (be it Saul or Achish); and in both these psalms David presses into his deliverance: the fear of the Lord. Just listen to his words:

> I sought the LORD, and He answered me; He delivered me *from all my fears.* ... The angel of the LORD encamps around those who *fear Him*;

and He delivers them. ... *Fear the LORD*, you His saints, for those who *fear Him* lack nothing. ... Come, my children, listen to me; I will teach you the *fear of the LORD*. ... (Psalm 34:4,7,9,11)

When I am *afraid*, I will trust in You. In God, *whose word I praise*, in God I trust; *I will not be afraid*. What can mortal man do to me? ... In God, *whose word I praise*, in the LORD, *whose word I praise*—in God I trust; *I will not be afraid*. What can man do to me? (Psalm 56: 3-4,10-11)

David, in these psalms, reveals to us four keys to his own quantum leap from fear to faith.

First, David began to *praise the Lord*. Praise is the language that faith speaks. Unbelief speaks language that is full of negative statements, doubts, fears, and discouragement. But faith praises God! Just listen to David: "I will *extol the LORD at all times*; His *praise will always* be on my lips. My soul will *boast in the LORD*. ... *Glorify the Lord* with me; let us *exalt His name* together" (Ps. 34:1-3). By God's grace, we must discipline ourselves to trade our language of unbelief for the language of faith!

Second, David set his heart to *seek the Lord*. Possibly in the initial quiet of the cave of Adullam, David closed himself in from all the jangling, confusing noises of earth, and simply sought the face of the Lord—in His Word, in waiting, in prayer, in praise, in composing these psalms. "I *sought the LORD*, and He answered me. ...those who *seek the LORD* lack no good thing" (Ps. 34:4a,10b). We too must shut ourselves in and set ourselves to seek His face!

Third, David *washed himself in the Word of God.*
David had undoubtedly committed to memory much of the
existent Scripture of that time, for now he declared: "In
God, *whose word I praise*, in God I trust; I will not be
afraid. What can mortal man do to me?" (Ps. 56:4; it is
repeated twice again in 56:10: "In God, *whose word I
praise*, in the LORD, *whose word I praise*....")

If praise is the *language* of our faith, then the Word of
God is surely the *fuel* for our faith. To strengthen faith, we
must wash ourselves in the Word of God; we must recount
again and again the nearly 40,000 promises of God—*all of
which* are for us as His new covenant people, "For no
matter how many promises God has made, they are *'Yes'* in
Christ. And so through Him the 'Amen' is spoken by us to
the glory of God" (2 Cor. 1:20). This powerful Pauline
statement tells us that behind every promise in God's Word
stands the "*Yes*" of Jesus. Consequently, we glorify God
when, through our Lord Jesus, we add our "*Amen*," our "so
be it" of faith, to every one of these promises of God!

Fourth, David superimposed upon his craven fear of
man the greater reverential fear of God. That makes perfect
sense. For what, exactly, "*can* man do to me" when I am
hidden in the hollow of the hands of the Sovereign, omnip-
otent God? (see Ps. 56: 3-4,10-11) In this David encourag-
es us from his own experience: "*Fear the LORD*, you His
saints, for those who *fear Him* lack nothing" (Ps. 34:9).

I look with deep compassion on David, just a young
man in his twenties at this stage in his life. But he has
begun to learn the greatest lesson any man or woman can

ever learn: "The LORD is *close* to the *brokenhearted* and saves those who are *crushed* in spirit" (Ps. 34:18). David is learning Paul Billheimer's lesson: "If God is going to perfect Christlikeness in you and in me, it may sometimes involve the failure of our ambitions, of our plans, of our dreams, of our hopes... *Failure is sometimes better than success!*"

Taking a Step of Faith

My dear Father, You see the fears of my heart. You see how I have become ensnared by the fear of man. I now renounce that "spirit of fear" in the almighty name of Jesus! I release, by faith, from deep within my being, that spring of praise to rise up to You! I set myself to seek Your face, and I will discipline myself, by Your grace, to speak Your faith-promises in the place of all the negative words that have come from my mouth. This day I take my quantum leap from fear to faith! In Jesus' name. Amen.

Day Nine

From the Ridiculous
to the Sublime

▶ Scripture Reading: 1 Samuel 22:1-5
Psalms 57 and 142

*Day after day men came to help David, until he had **a great army, like the army of God**."*
1 Chronicles 12:22

In my devotional reading over the years, I took special note of the following words from Mrs. Charles E. Cowman's inspiring devotional *Springs in the Valley*. These have been meaningful to me in my own walk with God, and they fit where we find ourselves today in the narrative of David's life:

The bird rises against a strong head wind, not only in spite of the wind, but *because of it*. The *opposing force* becomes a *lifting force* if faced at the right angle. The storm may buffet ships and rend the rigging, but... 'Spread thy sails to catch the

winds of adversity.'   Take the hardest thing in
your life—the place of difficulty, outward or
inward—and expect God to triumph gloriously *in
that very spot.*[4]

That very spot for David was the cave of Adullam—a hidden
cavern in the barren cliffs of the arid wilderness of Judah.
Tradition places Adullam six miles southeast of Bethlehem,
David's birthplace, near the Dead Sea. The mouth of the
cave is approachable only by foot across the cliff's edge.
The cave contains a large chamber with high arches and a
labyrinth of many passages spiraling off in all directions
from the main chamber. The air in the cave is dry and
pure. It would be at Adullam that David could "expect God
to triumph gloriously *in that very spot.*"

First Samuel 22:1-2 tells us that "David left Gath and
escaped to the cave of Adullam. When his brothers and his
father's household heard about it, they went down to him
there. All those who were in distress or in debt or discontented gathered around him, and he became their leader.
About four hundred men were with him."   The New
American Standard Bible seems to emphasize even more
strongly that "*everyone* who was in distress, and *everyone*
who was in debt, and *everyone* who was discontented
[literally, *everyone* who was bitter of soul] gathered to
him...." If anything, the cave of Adullam was another
illustration of Paul's evaluation of the Corinthians:

Brothers, think of what you were when you were
called. Not many of you were wise by human
standards; not many were influential; not many

were of noble birth. But God chose *the foolish* things of the world to shame the wise; God chose *the weak* things of the world to shame the strong. He chose *the lowly* things of the world and *the despised* things—and *the things that are not*—to nullify the things that are, so that no one may boast before Him" (1 Cor. 1:26-29).

The key to transformation for the Corinthians was that "Christ Jesus...has become *for us* wisdom from God—that is, our righteousness, holiness and redemption. Therefore, as it is written: 'Let him who boasts boast in the Lord'" (1 Cor. 1:30-31). What a marvelous testimony!

David's cave of Adullam, along with the Corinthian church, is a beautiful example of how the Lord is able to transform the lives of hurting, needy, broken people by His sovereign grace. It is "in that very spot" that God longs to triumph gloriously.

Speaking of church growth, it appears as if David's ragtag band of 400 men experienced a 50 percent growth rate that very first year! There were 600 men gathered around David at Keilah, an area close to Adullam, before the year was out (see 1 Sam. 23:13). The band just continued to multiply. First Chronicles 12 tells us of "the men who came to David at Ziklag [another town in the south country], while he was banished from the presence of Saul son of Kish." We are told that these "were among the warriors who helped him in battle": men who defected from Saul's tribe of Benjamin; some men from Gad; others from Benjamin and Judah; and some men from Manasseh.

Finally men came to David from all the tribes of Israel "until he had a great army, *like the army of God*"—over a third of a million strong! What a marvelous transformation! From debt-ridden and distressed and discontented to *divine*—the veritable army of God!

I have so come to love this statement in First Corinthians 1:30 "Christ Jesus...has become *for us* wisdom from God—that is, our righteousness, holiness and redemption"! His replaced life in us and for us and through us has become the secret to *our own* transformation into the army of God!

I remember the beginnings of Immanuel's Church in 1983; we were a little handful of people gathered in our family room, "the red room," on Springloch Road in Silver Spring, Maryland. A number in that little band—our own family included—were broken, beleaguered, battered, and bitter of soul. Some had been crushed by the wheels of religious politics; others had been broken by their own sin and by the circumstances of life. One day, in preparation for our simple Sunday afternoon breaking-of-bread meeting, I hung a humorous sign on our front door: "Welcome to the Cave of Adullam." Little did I realize that my sign was prophetic. The small band grew and grew and continued to grow until it outgrew all of its successive meeting places. Now, as I look out on Sundays on a congregation that includes more than 1,800 people (if everybody could come at once), I see "a great army, like the army of God"! I see a people who in themselves are often the "are not's" of First Corinthians 1:28, but who in Christ Jesus have become the very "righteousness of God" (2 Cor. 5:21). Yes, "take the hardest thing in your life—the place of difficulty, outward or inward—and expect God to triumph gloriously *in that very spot.*"[5]

Two psalms come down to us from David's heart describing the Adullam transformation from the ridiculous to the sublime. First there is Psalm 57 ("When he had fled from Saul into the cave") and then there is Psalm 142 ("When he was in the cave"). In these songs we find keys to the transformation David experienced for himself and the transformation he saw happen in others.

In Psalm 57 David describes for us his impossible circumstances; he speaks of "those who hotly pursue me" (verse 3) and those who "dug a pit in my path" (verse 6). Then, perhaps, he even sketches for us the ragtag 400 in their initial broken, battered, and bitter state at Adullam when he writes, "I am in the midst of lions; I lie among ravenous beasts—men whose teeth are spears and arrows, whose tongues are sharp swords" (verse 4).

The key of David (mentioned for us in Revelation 3:7), the key that David used to unlock this utterly impossible situation, was *high praise.* In Psalm 57 David declares:

I will take refuge in the shadow of Your wings until the disaster has passed. ... I will sing and make music. Awake, my soul! Awake, harp and lyre! I will awaken the dawn. I will praise You, O LORD, among the nations; I will sing of You among the peoples. For great is Your love, reaching to the heavens; Your faithfulness reaches to

the skies. Be exalted, O God, above the heavens;
let Your glory be over all the earth" (Psalm
57:1,7-11).

As the first rays of dawn stretched above the horizon,
David was filling the cave of Adullam with praises to his
God. On his stringed instruments and with his melodic
voice David magnified Israel's Redeemer!

Similarly, in Psalm 142 David pours out his sorrows
before Jehovah:

> ...men have hidden a snare for me. ... no one is
> concerned for me. I have no refuge; no one cares
> for my life. ... "You are my refuge, my portion in
> the land of the living." Listen to my cry, for I am
> in desperate need; rescue me from those who
> pursue me, for they are too strong for me. Set me
> free from my prison, *that I may praise Your name.*
> Then the righteous will gather about me because
> of Your goodness to me (Psalm 142:3-7).

Can't you just see David, rising in faith over and above
all his negative circumstances on the wings of praise to His
God? Then look and see how infectious David's faith in
Jehovah has become; see the bitter, the broken, and the
battered who surround him, themselves now responding to
the redeeming covenant love of Jehovah and being made
whole! Whereas the men who once surrounded David were
"men whose teeth are spears and arrows, whose tongues are
sharp swords," those very men, I believe, are now "the
righteous" who gathered about David because of Jehovah's
goodness to him! From these hundreds of distressed, bitter

malcontents, Jehovah begins to create an army like the very army of God! Indeed, "Take the hardest thing in your life—the place of difficulty, outward or inward—and expect God to triumph gloriously *in that very spot*!"

Taking a Step of Faith

Lord Jesus, You find me standing this day in wits-end corner. I am pressed on every side. I am crushed by the pressure of merciless circumstances. But I choose to bring to You my sacrifice of praise. I bless You! I extol You! I glorify Your name! Great is Your love, reaching to the heavens, and Your faithfulness, reaching to the skies! I believe You will work the wonders of Your delivering, redeeming grace this very day in my circumstances. In Your dear name I pray. Amen.

Day Ten

The Pain of Betrayal

▶ Scripture Reading: 1 Samuel 23

Surely God is my help; the LORD is the one who sustains me.

Psalm 54:4

The pain of betrayal is an especially hurtful emotional pain. The word *betray* comes from the Latin *tradere*, "to hand over." The word carries the meaning of helping the enemy, delivering or exposing one to the enemy, breaking faith with one, or trading one off. Betrayal is, therefore, emotionally painful to bear, especially when we are betrayed by loved ones, friends, or those whom we have sought to help.

We have seen in First Samuel 21 and 22 David's betrayal by Doeg the Edomite and the fatal consequences of that betrayal on an innocent community of men, women, and children. But then, David had apparently not meant much to Doeg; no trust had been established between them.

In First Samuel 23, however, we are introduced to a more painful betrayal: the betrayal of David by the men of Keilah. Keilah was a small but well-fortified town in the *shephelah*, or lowland hills of Judah, just south of Adullam. *Keilah* means "fortress"; the city entrance was secured as a fortress "with double gates and bars" (1 Sam. 23:7 NASB). Keilah's high-security system served as a protection against invaders like the Philistines. As chapter 23 opens, we overhear a military briefing being given to David: "Look, the Philistines are fighting against Keilah and are looting the threshing floors," plundering the year's harvest. David's response to the report was that twice (the second time because of the fearful reservations of his men) "he inquired of the LORD, saying, 'Shall I go and attack these Philistines?'" The LORD's word to David, given through the Urim and Thumim (see 1 Sam. 23:6,9), was "Go, attack the Philistines and save Keilah...for I am going to give the Philistines into your hand." This Jehovah did. "So David and his men went to Keilah [and] fought the Philistines.... He inflicted heavy losses on the Philistines and saved the people of Keilah" (1 Sam. 23:5). Thus David was hero for a day, Keilah's champion!

Saul, hearing that David was in Keilah, then marched on the town to besiege it and kill David. David, hearing that Saul's armies were approaching Keilah, again inquired twice of Jehovah, asking a most painful question: "Will the citizens of Keilah surrender me and my men to Saul?" The hurtful answer was given: "They will." So it was that "David and his men, about six hundred in number, left Keilah and kept moving from place to place.... David stayed in the desert strongholds and in the hills of the

Desert of Ziph. Day after day Saul searched for him, *but God* did not give David into his hands" (1 Sam. 23:13-14).

There are good grounds to believe that Psalm 31 comes to us from the sorrow that filled David's heart as he reflected on his betrayal by the men of Keilah, the men whose very fortunes he had saved. Psalm 31 also prophetically resonates with the anguish of the Son of Man, betrayed by both a calculating Judas and a cowardly Peter, then abandoned to His enemies by all those closest to Him.

> In You, O LORD, I have taken refuge; let me never be put to shame...be my rock of refuge. ... Free me from the trap that is set for me, for You are my refuge. *Into your hands I commit my spirit.* ... I will be glad and rejoice in Your love, for You saw my affliction and knew the anguish of my soul. You have not handed me over to the enemy but have set my feet in a spacious place. ... Let Your face shine on Your servant; save me in Your unfailing love. ... Praise be to the LORD, for He showed His wonderful love to me when I was in a besieged city. ... Love the LORD, all His saints! The LORD preserves the faithful.... Be strong and take heart, all you who hope in the LORD (Psalm 31:1-2,4-5,7-8,16-21,23-24).

Here we see the deep anguish of David's soul being healed by the "unfailing love," the "wonderful love" of His wonderful God!

Before this 23rd chapter of First Samuel closes, David will be betrayed yet again—this time by the Ziphites, who gladly promised David to Saul: "We will be responsible for handing him over to the king" (1 Sam. 23:20). Saul would have had David in his hands that day, but the Lord used another Philistine raiding party to distract him, so "Saul broke off his pursuit of David and went to meet the Philistines" (1 Sam. 23:28).

In Psalm 54 David celebrates the Lord's deliverances "when the Ziphites had gone to Saul and said, 'Is not David hiding among us?'" David had cried to his heavenly Father, "Strangers are attacking me; ruthless men seek my life—men without regard for God" (Ps. 54:3). Then he testified, "Surely God is my help; the LORD is the one who sustains me. ... For He has delivered me from all my troubles, and my eyes have looked in triumph on my foes" (Ps. 54:4,7). Indeed, *the Lord is the one* who delivered David!

In the very heart of First Samuel 23, in the midst of betrayal on every side, David has a most gratifying experience, which comes to him as a cup of cool water in a dry and weary land. We are told that "while David was at Horesh in the Desert of Ziph," an area yet further south in the wild and untamed hill country of Judah, "Jonathan went to David at Horesh and *helped him find strength in God*" (1 Sam. 23:15-16). This expression in the Hebrew is "strengthened his hand in God." Jonathan "encouraged him in God" (NASB); he put fresh heart into David his covenant brother, his beloved friend. In the course of their sharing, Prince Jonathan (heir to his father Saul's throne) speaks from his heart: "Don't be afraid," he says. "My father Saul will not lay a hand on you. *You will be king over Israel*, and I will be second to you" (1 Sam. 23:17). If we have ever wondered what it means to "lay down our lives for our brothers" (1 Jn. 3:16), we see a clear demonstration of that here. We see in Jonathan a beautiful reflection of the self-sacrificing love of our dear Lord Jesus. "He laid down His life for us" as Jonathan laid down his life for David, and as we are to lay down our lives for one another!

Psalm 63, written by David "when he was in the Desert of Judah," is a celebration of this happy reunion between himself and Jonathan. Just listen to David's faith-filled words as he reflected on those precious moments with Jonathan:

> O God, You are my God, earnestly I seek You; my soul thirsts for You, my body longs for You, in a dry and weary land where there is no water. ... I will praise You as long as I live, and in Your name *I will lift up my hands* ['And Jonathan... strengthened his hand in God' (KJV)]. ... On my bed I remember You; I think of You through the watches of the night. ...I sing in the shadow of Your wings. My soul clings to You. ... *They who seek my life will be destroyed*; ['Don't be afraid. My father Saul will not lay a hand on you']... *But the king will rejoice in God* ['You will be king over Israel, and I will be second to you']; *all who swear by God's name* will praise Him ['The two of them made covenant before the LORD']... (Psalm 63:1,4,6-7,9,11; see also 1 Samuel 23:16-18).

David thanked God that night on his bed for Jonathan, as he pressed close to the heart of Jehovah, his God! The pain of betrayal had been lifted in some degree by the loyalty of his dearest friend.

Taking a Step of Faith

Lord Jesus, You know the broken places in my heart—places broken by the betrayal of even those who had been close to me. You have been there Yourself, my Master. I thank You for friendships that heal; above all else, I thank You for Your friendship that heals. I receive Your "wonderful love," Your "unfailing love" this day, my Redeemer and my God! In Your dear name I pray. Amen.

Day Eleven

Marks of True Greatness

▶ Scripture Reading: 1 Samuel 24 and 26

Then Saul said to David, "Blessed are you, my son David; you will both accomplish much and surely prevail."

1 Samuel 26:25 NASB

For many years I have carried this poem by Angela Morgan in my Bible; it is one of my favorites.

> When God wants to drill a man,
> And thrill a man, and skill a man;
> When God wants to mold a man
> To play the noblest part;
> When He yearns with all His heart
> To create so great and bold a man
> That all the world shall be amazed
> Watch His methods; watch His ways:
> How He ruthlessly perfects
> Whom He royally elects!

> How He hammers him and hurts him,
> And with mighty blows converts him
> Into trial shapes of clay
> Which God only understands;
> While his tortured heart is crying,
> And he lifts beseeching hands!
> How He bends but never breaks
> When his good He undertakes.
> How He uses whom He chooses,
> And with every purpose fuses him
> But every act induces him
> To try His splendor out ...
> God *knows* *what He's about!*

In our Scriptures for today, we will see the out-workings of this poem. The disciplines of God were impressing their marks on David—marks of true greatness.

The previous chapter of David's life closes at "the strongholds [the inaccessible places] of En Gedi" (1 Sam. 23:29). In the fall of 1979, while on pilgrimage in Israel, I had my introduction to this delightful Judean spring of En Gedi, "the spring of the kid," just west of the Dead Sea at the threshold of the wilderness of Judah. There between the deadness of the ancient Salt Sea and the bleak and barren Judean desert are nestled the sparkling waterfall, refreshing pool, and flowing stream of En Gedi, all surrounded by rich greenery—the lair of wild animals and the nesting place of birds. Here David, as a hunted animal and as a stalked bird, sought refuge from Saul. But soon

Saul would be told that David was in the Desert of En Gedi. So Saul mustered 3,000 choice men from Israel and set out to search for David and his men near a place called the "Crags of the Wild Goats."

In the course of his march, Saul made a needed latrine call, pulling aside and entering a cave near some sheep-folds. Unknown to Saul, David and some of his men were hiding in the inner recesses of that very cave! As Saul relieved and refreshed himself, possibly even dozing off in the process, David stealthily crept up to him and quietly cut off a piece from the edge of his robe. David's men hoped that he would take the opportunity and actually kill Saul, believing that the Lord had given the enemy into David's hand, but David could not find it in his heart even to touch the Lord's anointed. Not only could he not kill Saul, but David was conscience-stricken for cutting off even a corner of his robe! The ability to forgive; the holy art of being able to entrust a grave injustice into the hands of a faithful God; the respect for the anointing of God even when it has nearly faded from an adversary's life—these are marks of true greatness. These are the fruits of spiritual maturity. This is evidence of the deeper dealings of God within a man's soul.

When Saul was a safe distance away, David called out to him and disclosed all that had just happened and all that *could* have just happened. Saul's astonishing prophetic response to David was, "You are more righteous than I.... May the Lord reward you well for the way you treated me today. I know that you will surely be king and that the kingdom of Israel will be established in your hands" (1 Sam. 24:17,19-20)! Saul saw in David, even through his dimmed prophetic eyes, the marks of royal greatness. And so they parted. Saul returned home—his crown rusting, his prophetic anointing fading, his days numbered. David and his mighty men returned to their wilderness stronghold. David returned more deeply affirmed in Jehovah's holy character, bearing the marks of kingly greatness. The cries of his soul are reflected in his words:

> Commit your way to the LORD; trust in Him and He will do this: He will make your righteousness shine like the dawn, the justice of your cause like the noonday sun. ... The salvation of the righteous comes from the LORD; He is their stronghold in time of trouble. The LORD helps them and delivers them; He delivers them from the wicked and saves them, because they take refuge in Him (Psalm 37:5-6, 39-40).

In First Samuel 26 the Ziphites, for the second time, betrayed David to Saul, revealing David's whereabouts in their territory. Saul, again stirred to do evil and accompanied by 3,000 foot soldiers, marched on David's position at the hill of Hakilah. As nightfall came, Saul's army made camp. David again stealthily crept up on a sleeping Saul, this time accompanied by Abishai, his faithful nephew, the brother of Joab, his war-chief. Standing near the sleeping Saul, Abishai's whispered words to David were pointed and convincing: "Today God has delivered your enemy into your hands. Now let me pin him to the ground with one thrust of my spear; I won't strike him twice" (1 Sam. 26:8). But again David refused to harm Saul, whom he yet saw as "Jehovah's anointed." He chose rather to only take Saul's spear and his water jug as proof of his midnight visit. At a safe distance, David called out to Saul and disclosed all that had happened and likewise all that *could* have happened. A broken Saul, again seeing the greatness of David's heart, could only cry out, "May you be blessed, my son David; you will do great things and surely triumph" (1 Sam. 26:25). And so the two parted, this time for the final time—Saul the fool and David the prince. The next time David heard of Saul was when the men of Jabash Gilead recovered Saul's decapitated body from the wall of Beth Shan and cremated it, along with the bodies of his three sons (Jonathan, David's beloved friend, and Jonathan's two brothers, Abinadab and Malki-Shua). Saul's concluding testimony and the epitaph on his whole life was "I have played the fool" (1 Sam. 26:21 KJV). David's concluding testimony at Ziph was: "Surely God is my help; the LORD is the one who sustains me. ... For He has delivered me from all my troubles, and my eyes have looked in triumph on my foes" (Ps. 54:4,7). Two men, David and Saul, were a spiritual son and a spiritual father—the one a truly great man, the other a fool; the one destined to shine as the brightness of the stars forever, the other consigned to shame and everlasting contempt. Two men had the same anointing, but one was untried, unbent, unbroken, and eventually overthrown; the other was drilled and skilled and molded, royally elected and ruthlessly perfected. David carried the marks of true greatness!

Taking a Step of Faith

*Father, I understand more clearly something of Your puzzling ways within my life—how You ruthlessly perfect whom You royally elect. While I resist, in Jesus' name, all the workings of my enemy, I do accept, in Jesus' name, all **Your** workings. Drill me, thrill me, skill me, mold me! I unreservedly yield myself to You for Jesus' sake. I would bear the marks of true greatness. Amen.*

Day Twelve

A Root of Unresolved Anger

▶ Scripture Reading: 1 Samuel 25

Refrain from anger and turn from wrath; do not fret—it leads only to evil. For evil men will be cut off, but those who hope in the LORD will inherit the land.

Psalm 37:8-9

Anger is often an expression of unresolved hurt, the venting of pain from unhealed wounds. Rage is often the breaking out of hurt and pain that have been unaddressed and stuffed down deep within the human soul. When we look at David's outbursts of rage and anger, faithfully recorded for us in the Holy Scriptures, we sense the erupting of broken emotions that may well go back to his youth. Here is a young man wrestling with the liability of his Moabite ancestry, the uncertainty of his birth, the rejection of his mother and father (see Ps. 27:10), the estrangement and alienation of his brothers (see Ps, 69:8), the loss of his spiritual hero and father Saul, and the devastation of losing his loving wife Michal (whom Saul, in an act of spite, had given as a wife "to Palti the son of Laish, who was from Gallim" [1 Sam. 25:44 NASB]). These are pains and hurts for which no balm had yet been found by David in Gilead.

Even in his more mature years David wrestled with anger. When Uzzah was struck by the Lord for his irreverence toward the ark of Jehovah's Presence, David's initial response was that he "became angry because of the LORD's outburst against Uzzah..." (2 Sam. 6:8 NASB). In reporting the account of Israel's defeat at Rabbah, the messenger feared that "the king's anger may flare up" (2 Sam. 11:19-20). When the judgments of God took David and Bathsheba's firstborn son, David's servants feared telling him the news, declaring that "he may do something desperate" (2 Sam. 12:18). When David learned of his son Amnon's violation of his half-sister Tamar, "he was furious" (2 Sam. 13:21). In our reading for today from First Samuel 25, we are introduced to David's heated anger in his confrontation with the wealthy fool from Maon, Nabal. Nabal's wife, Abigail, is described as "a beautiful and very intelligent woman," but Nabal himself is pictured as "uncouth, churlish, stubborn, and ill-mannered" (1 Sam. 25:3 TLB).

David and his 600 warriors living in the wilderness surrounding Maon had been a wall of protection for Nabal's shepherds and for Nabal's extensive flocks. For this service, David sent to Nabal asking for a little contribution—some bread and water and meat for their sustenance. Nabal's rebuff of David's request angered David.

"Get your swords!" was David's quick and heated response as he strapped on his own sword and took off with 400 of his men to confront Nabal. David's intent was to kill Nabal and his entire band of ranch hands that very night! Only the interception of the gracious Abigail—en route with 200 loaves of bread, 2 skins of wine, 5 dressed sheep, a bushel of roasted grain, 100 raisin cakes, and 200 fig cakes—prevented the carnage. Abigail's pleas to David to reconsider his vengeful plan were heeded, and in the aftermath David praised God for her wisdom and kindness. "Bless the Lord God of Israel who has sent you to meet me today," he told Abigail. "Thank God for your good sense! Bless you for keeping me from murdering the man and carrying out vengeance with my own hands" (1 Sam. 25:32-33 TLB).

Perhaps with Nabal in mind, David admonished his people: "Refrain from anger and turn from wrath...it leads only to evil. For evil men *will* be cut off, but those who hope in the LORD will inherit the land. A little while, and the wicked will be no more; through you look for them, they will not be found" (Ps. 37:8-10). Within days the fool Nabal died of a stroke. The Lord had struck him down, and David's response was full of gratitude and praise: "Praise be to the LORD, who has upheld my cause against Nabal for treating me with contempt. He has kept his servant from doing wrong and has brought Nabal's wrongdoing down on his own head..." (1 Sam. 25:39).

Solomon, as seen in his wisdom writings, undoubtedly reflected on his father David's growing awareness that "a hot-tempered man stirs up dissension, but a patient man calms a quarrel" (Prov. 15:18). "Better a patient man than a warrior, a man who controls his temper than one who takes a city" (Prov. 16:32). "Do not be quickly provoked in your spirit, for anger resides in the lap of fools" (Eccles. 7:9). David had undoubtedly impressed his peace-loving son Solomon with a respect for patience and calmness of spirit.

Those of us who have struggled with anger in our own lives are obligated to place ourselves under the searchlight of God's Holy Spirit as David did in Psalm 139. David first took an honest look at the sinful feelings that lay buried within his own heart against others: "I hate them with the utmost hatred; they have become my enemies." David then cried out to God: "Search me, O God, and know my heart; try me and know my anxious thoughts; and see if there be any hurtful way [literally, 'any way of pain'] in me, and lead me in the everlasting way" (Ps. 139:22-24 NASB). I must believe that as David allowed the searchlight of God's Holy Spirit to shine in his heart, the Lord began to heal his crushed spirit and mend his broken heart, and then instructed him how to control his temper. Fanny Crosby, that great blind gospel songwriter, assures us in her hymn—"Rescue the Perishing:"

> Down in the human heart,
> Crushed by the tempter,
> Feelings lie buried that grace can restore;
> Touched by a loving hand,
> Wakened by kindness,
> Chords that were broken will vibrate once more.

So we, too, must believe God for this work of His grace within our own hearts.

> Keep me from wrath, let it seem ever so right:
> My wrath will never work Thy righteousness.
> Up, up the hill, to the whiter than snow-shine,
> Help me to climb, and dwell in pardon's light.
> I must be pure as Thou, or ever less
> Than Thy design of me—therefore incline
> My heart to take men's wrongs as Thou tak'st mine.
>
>   George MacDonald[6]

Taking a Step of Faith

Father, I ask You, as David did, to "search me...and know my heart; try me and know my anxious thoughts." Look inside me and see if there be any way of pain within me. I trust You to restore by Your grace crushed feelings that lie buried within me, to touch those broken chords with Your own gentle hands, and to cause my inner being to resonate with Your peace and joy! Lead me in the everlasting way. I believe You can enable me to walk out of my brokenness into Your wholeness! For Jesus' sake. Amen.

Day Thirteen

Seasons of Great Loss

▶ Scripture Reading: 1 Samuel 30 and 31

David was greatly distressed.... But David found strength in the LORD his God."

1 Samuel 30:6

There are seasons in our lives that are seasons of great loss. We suffer the loss of loved ones; we suffer the loss of our mentors and our heroes; we suffer the loss of our reputations and our places of service. In the final chapters of First Samuel we come upon just such a time in David's life; now in his late twenties, he will sustain repeated and great personal losses. In the midst of these personal tragedies, David will walk the length and the breadth of the truth penned by Rudyard Kipling:

> If you can meet with triumph and disaster
> And treat those two impostors just the same;
> If you can bear to hear the truth you've spoken
> Twisted by knaves to make a trap for fools,

Or watch the things you gave your life to broken,
And stop and build them up with worn out tools ...
Yours is the earth and everything that's in it,
And—what is more—you'll be a man, my son!

We have already taken note of one of David's severest losses: the loss of his wife, Michal, for "Saul had given his daughter Michal, David's wife, to Paltiel son of Laish, who was from Gallim" (1 Sam. 25:44). Just after the untimely death of Nabal the fool, struck down by Jehovah's own hand, David took Nabal's wife, the lovely Abigail, to be his own wife. Abigail means "source of joy," and this she was to David in the loss of Michal. Indeed, "a wife of noble character who can find? She is worth far more than rubies" (Prov. 31:10).

In First Samuel 25:1, we are also told that "Samuel died, and all Israel assembled and mourned for him; and they buried him at his home in Ramah." The man who had anointed David (and Saul before him), the man who was David's mentor and a strength to him, now lay cold in death at Ramah. Samuel's death was a great loss to David. Saul, a man of infinitely less spirituality than David, went right over the edge after Samuel's death. His grave sin of consulting the medium at Endor (recorded in First Samuel 28) was his frantic attempt to establish contact with the departed Samuel after his death. But in the midst of this great personal loss, David himself clung to the Lord his God as his strength and his shield.

In First Samuel 30, we are allowed to share the pain of yet another great loss in David's life: the loss sustained at

Ziklag. The Philistine city of Ziklag had been given to David as a refuge by Achish, the King of Gath. Here David lived for nearly a year and a half, exiled from his people and from his land—a stranger in the country of the Philistines. In Ziklag David and his men lived with their families; this was their home base as they went out on raiding parties against the Geshurites and the Girzites and the Amalekites. During these days, David and his men were nearly drafted into the Philistine army as the Philistines advanced to make their fatal attack on Saul and the armies of Israel, but the Lord sovereignly spared David from participating in this bloodguiltiness. However, as David and his men returned to Ziklag after being dismissed from the army of Achish, they found that in their absence the Amalekites had raided Ziklag and burned it with fire, taking all the women, the children, and the livestock. This was a crushing loss for David. Amidst the smoldering ruins of Ziklag, "David and his men wept aloud until they had no strength left to weep" (1 Sam. 30:4). Besides the pain of his own personal losses, "David was greatly distressed because the men were talking of stoning him; each one was bitter in spirit because of his sons and daughters. But David found strength in the LORD his God" (1 Sam. 30:6). David strengthened himself in the Lord; he encouraged himself in Jehovah! Then David inquired of the Lord, who assured him of victory against these raiders. So David and his men pursued and overtook the Amalekites; slaughtered them and "recovered everything the Amalekites had taken.... Nothing was missing.... David brought everything back" (1 Sam. 30:18-19). And so Ziklag became the scene of a triumph, for David shared these spoils with the elders of the various cities of Judah that the Amalekites had raided. We are told in First Chronicles 12:1 of all "the men who came to David at Ziklag, while he was banished from the presence of Saul son of Kish (they were among the warriors who helped him in battle)." It was here, in this very place of deepest loss, that God would begin to build David's great army, an army "like the army of God" (1 Chron. 12:22).

In First Samuel 31, David sustained a final blow—the great loss of his dearest friend Jonathan, slain with his father Saul on Mount Gilboa. There the Philistines killed Jonathan and his two brothers and wounded Saul, who then took his own life by falling on his sword. We are told in First Chronicles 10:13-14, however, that "Saul died because he was unfaithful to the LORD; he did not keep the word of the LORD and even consulted a medium for guidance, and did not inquire of the LORD. So *the LORD put him to death* and turned the kingdom over to David son of Jesse."

Valiant men secured the bodies of Saul and his three sons from the wall of Beth Shan, where the Philistines had impaled them. These men then cremated their remains at Jabesh and buried their bones under a nearby tamarisk tree. David later reverently removed these remains and had them buried in Saul's family plot at Zela in Benjamin (see 2 Sam. 21:12-14).

The anguished cries of David over the loss of his dearest friend Jonathan echo in our ears from the mountains of Gilboa: "I grieve for you, Jonathan my brother; you

were very dear to me. Your love for me was wonderful..."
(2 Sam. 1:26).

At this juncture of his life, David could well have
penned these words of the great apostle Paul: "...I consider
everything a loss compared to the surpassing greatness of
knowing Christ Jesus my Lord, for whose sake I have lost
all things.... I want to know Christ and the power of His
resurrection and the fellowship of sharing in His sufferings..." (Phil. 3:8,10). So it is by the grace of God that we
can emerge out of our seasons of great loss with spoils and
with great gains, the greatest gain being more of our Lord
Jesus Christ!

In a time of personal crisis some 14 years ago, it
seemed as if we as a family sustained the loss of all things.
All our friends, with very few exceptions, left us. Our
mentors and our heroes were gone; our reputation and our
place of ministry were lost to us. At that time our only
promise from the Lord was David's words: "He reached
down from on high and took hold of me; He drew me out
of deep waters. ... He brought me out into a spacious
place; He rescued me because He delighted in me" (Ps.
18:16,19). Our passion became "to know Christ and the
power of His resurrection and the fellowship of sharing in
His sufferings"; our joy was in reckoning "everything a loss
compared to the surpassing greatness of knowing Christ
Jesus [our] Lord...." (Phil. 3:10,8). And the Lord brought
us out into a spacious place! We all invariably will know
seasons of great loss, but in those seasons we shall come to
find Him, our greatest gain!

Taking a Step of Faith

*Father, You know the losses I have sustained. Work within me that I may gladly consider **everything** a loss compared to the surpassing greatness of knowing Christ Jesus my Lord. I open wide my heart so that Jesus may be revealed in me; I want to know Him and share in His sufferings so that His powerful resurrection life might flow out of me! For His sake. Amen!*

Part Two

God Uses David,
His Chosen

Day Fourteen

Laughing for Wonder
and Delight

► Scripture Reading: 2 Samuel 2:1-4; 3:1; 4:1—5:5

...So the LORD...turned the kingdom over to David son of Jesse.

1 Chronicles 10:14

I can still believe that a day comes for all of us, however far off it may be, when we shall understand, when these tragedies that now blacken and darken the very air of heaven for us will sink into their places in a scheme so august, so magnificent, so joyful, that we shall laugh for wonder and delight (Arthur C. Benson).

The Benjamite Saul and his three eldest sons lay dead on Mount Gilboa. The foundations of the throne of Israel and Judah were shaken. Up from the valley of the shadow of death "...David brought up his men who were with him, each with his household; and they lived in the cities of

Hebron" (2 Sam. 2:3 NASB). David's seven long years of great personal tribulation were now over. The power of the oppressor had at last been broken. David celebrated his deliverance in the words of a "song to the LORD in the day that the LORD delivered him from the hand of all his enemies and from the hand of Saul" (2 Sam. 22:1 NASB). In this song, which we have previously touched on, David cried out, "I love Thee, O LORD, my strength. The LORD is my rock and my fortress and my deliverer, my God, my rock, in whom I take refuge; my shield and the horn of my salvation, my stronghold. I call upon the LORD; who is worthy to be praised, and I am saved from my enemies" (Ps. 18:1-3 NASB; cf. 2 Sam. 22 and Ps. 18). David had brought out of the wilderness crucible a deeper love for Jehovah and a collection of brand-new names, or word pictures, that he had coined for the Lord. All of them were memorials to the Lord's faithfulness to him in his wilderness experiences: my Rock, my Fortress, my Deliverer, my God, my Rock of refuge, my Shield, my Salvation, my Stronghold!

The men of Judah then came to Hebron to anoint David, now a full 30 years old, as the lion king of the tribe of Judah. And so began the fulfillment of Jacob's great messianic prophecy concerning Judah, the lion's whelp: "The scepter shall not depart from Judah, nor the ruler's staff from between his feet, until Shiloh [the Prince of Peace] comes, and to him shall be the obedience of the peoples" (Gen. 49:10 NASB).

It was yet another seven and a half years before all of the tribes of Israel recognized David as Jehovah's anointed king; seven and a half painful years of civil war—"a long

war between the house of Saul and the house of David"—
but in those years "David grew steadily stronger, but the
house of Saul grew weaker continually" (2 Sam. 3:1
NASB). Then finally, Abner, the general of the armies of
Israel, was murdered. Saul's one remaining son, Esh-Baal
(known also as Ish-Bosheth) also was assassinated, leaving
the northern tribes of Israel virtually decapitated. Only then
did all the tribes of Israel humbly come to David at Hebron
saying, "'Behold, we are your bone and your flesh.' ... So
all the elders of Israel came to the king at Hebron, and
King David made a covenant with them before the LORD at
Hebron; then they anointed David king over Israel" (2 Sam.
5:1,3 NASB). David had reigned over Judah for seven and
a half years; now he would reign over all the 12 tribes of
Israel for yet another 33 years until his seventieth year.

When David took his place on the throne as the lion
king over all the people of God, he inherited not much
more than 12 bands of ragtag nomads. These David would
forge into one of the mightiest empires of his day. David
had received from Saul's hands a diminished kingdom.
Saul, in all his wars, had actually lost more territory to the
Philistines than he had gained; the kingdom was smaller at
his death than when he first became king. (The disobedient
always seem to lose out in this very way to the enemy.)
But David would extend the borders of the kingdom and
make Israel one of the most formidable and expansive
empires of his time, extending from the eastern arm of the
Red Sea all the way north and east to the Euphrates River.
David would actually fulfill—for the first time in Israel's
history—the great commission given to Joshua by Jehovah.

I will give you every place where you set your foot,
as I promised Moses. Your territory will extend
from the desert [in the south] to Lebanon [in the
north], and from the great river, the Euphrates [in
the east]—all the Hittite country—to the Great Sea
[the Mediterranean] on the west. No one will be
able to stand up against you all the days of your
life. ...I will be with you; I will never leave you nor
forsake you (Joshua 1:3-5).

Just prior to the days of the reign of Saul, when the
elders of Israel first came to the prophet Samuel at Ramah
and said, "You are old, and your sons do not walk in your
ways; now appoint a king to lead us, such as all the other
nations have" (1 Sam. 8:5), we are told that Samuel was
displeased. Jehovah Himself felt deeply rejected. "It is
not you they have rejected, but Me," Jehovah told Samuel
(1 Sam. 8:7). It is apparent from this interaction that the
monarchy was not God's highest will; a human king ruling
over Israel was God's "second best." The failed monarchy
under Saul, son of Kish, was but an outworking of the
Lord's concerns. How, then, shall we understand Jehovah's
reactions to Israel's second king?   The Lord appeared
delighted with His appointment of David. Jehovah called
him, chose him, and anointed him with great excitement
and anticipation: "You will shepherd My people Israel, and
you will become their ruler" (1 Chron. 11:2)! As we read
the Lord's thoughts concerning David's kingship, we are
compelled to believe that the monarchy had now become
Jehovah's *highest* will, His *first* choice, His *best*! To what
can we attribute this seeming change in the Lord's thinking
(if we even dare to put the question that way)? The answer

lies in the fact that David was *a king after God's own heart* and that he exercised his leadership over Israel in such a fashion that Jehovah was *more* the king in the people's lives than ever before. David's reign *enhanced* the rule of Jehovah among God's people. David's one great passion was for Israel to be a theocracy— that Jehovah Himself would reign supreme over all and that the kingdom would be Jehovah's. "Yours, O LORD, is the greatness and the power and the glory and the majesty and the splendor, for everything in heaven and earth is yours. Yours, O LORD, is the kingdom; *You* are exalted as head over all" (1 Chron. 29:11). David's vast military conquests were for one purpose: that all the lands might be "*subject to the LORD and to His people*" (1 Chron. 22:18). When it was time for Solomon to ascend the throne, David reminded him that this was "the throne of the kingdom of the LORD over Israel" and that Solomon would sit "on the throne of the LORD as king in place of his father David" (1 Chron. 28:5; 29:23).

As I pondered the implications of this insight in view of my own leadership in the Body of Christ, my heart became greatly humbled before the Lord. I saw myself with an awesome responsibility in my leadership to enhance *the Lord's* leadership over His people, to see them coming more fully under *His* authority, to see them more clearly hearing *His* voice, and to see them following *Him* more passionately and more fully obeying *Him*. I could not, therefore, draw the people of God to myself, nor ever take that place in their lives that is reserved only for Him. Only in this way can any of us genuinely serve the purposes of our God in this generation and be servants after His own heart, servants who will do according to all His will!

Taking a Step of Faith

*Lord Jesus, You have entrusted me with the awesome responsibility of serving Your people. I laugh for wonder and delight at the service You have opened up for me. Now focus my eyes, sharpen my vision, and establish my heart in such a way that, as a result of my leadership, men and women will be all the more brought under **Your** leadership, under **Your** headship, under **Your** lordship. I pray this for Your sake, dear Lord Jesus. Amen.*

Day Fifteen

Taking the Fortress of Zion

▶ Scripture Reading: 2 Samuel 5:6-12
1 Chronicles 11:4-9

David captured the fortress of Zion, the City of David.

I Chronicles 11:5

An unknown poet writes:

> I would not lose the hard things from my life—
> The rocks o'er which I stumbled long ago,
> The griefs, the fears, the failures, the mistakes,
> That tried and tested faith and patience so.
> I need them now; they make the deep-laid wall,
> The firm foundation-stones on which I raise,
> To mount thereon from stair to stair,
> The lofty towers of my House of Praise.

Indeed, all of David's 37 years of life and experience now focus on the great beginning events of his 33 year reign as Israel's lion king from Judah. All of Israel had acknowledged David at Hebron as God's appointed shepherd over all 12 tribes of Israel. David would reign over all Israel for 33 more years, transforming it into Jehovah's empire, the kingdom of the Lord.

David's very first act as king was the conquest of the Jebusite city of Jerusalem. This ancient city of Salem stood dead center in the midst of the 12 tribes of Israel. Near the border of Judah and Benjamin, Jerusalem was situated midway between the ten tribes of Israel to the north and the southern two tribes over whom David initially had reigned for seven years. The city was just west of the Jordan River, positioned midway between Israel's western border on the Great Sea (the Mediterranean) and the eastern border of the tribes of Reuben, Gad, and Manasseh. The name *Jerusalem* means "foundation" (*Jeru*) "of peace" (*shalem*). Zion, as it was also called, was the impregnable fortress of the Jebusites, a highly fortified prominence between the Kidron and the Tryopean Valleys. Second Chronicles 3:1 also reveals this site to be the sacred area of Mount Moriah, where Abraham offered up Isaac in obedience to Jehovah (see Gen. 22:2), and First Samuel 17:54 identifies this ground as the place where David, as a young lad, had taken the skull of Goliath of Gath—"the Place of the Skull," Golgotha (see Mt. 27:33). Genesis 14 also identifies this city as the city of the mysterious Melchizedek, the "King of Righteousness," the King of Salem, that is, the "King of Peace." Melchizedek, the priest of El Elyon, priest of *God Most High*, is presented to us as a prefigurement or possibly even as a preincarnation of our Lord Jesus Christ or both. Jerusalem is eventually hailed by the sons of Korah in Psalm 48 as "the city of our God, His holy mountain."

Mount Zion is called by them "the city of the Great King [for] God is in her citadels; He has shown Himself to be her fortress" (Ps. 48:1-3). This city David *must* have as his capital city, at any cost! Here Jehovah will reign, at the center of *His* kingdom, at the vortex of *His* empire!

From their lofty battlements the Jebusites initially resisted David and taunted him: "'You will not get in here; even the blind and the lame can ward you off.'... Nevertheless, David captured the fortress of Zion, the City of David" (2 Sam. 5: 6-7). The first to break through the Jebusite gates was Joab. So important was this conquest to David that he officially elevated Joab to be his primal war chief, the commander-in-chief of all Israel's armies.

In the days yet ahead, we will talk more about a most marvelous truth concerning David: he *functioned as a priest* in his worship and service of Jehovah! Like Jesus, who would follow him, David was denied access to the priesthood of God because he was not from Levi, but from Judah, "and in regard to that tribe Moses said nothing about priests" (Heb. 7:14). Furthermore, as a Moabite descendant, and because he possibly was illegitimate, David's family line might live in the land but could legally be denied access to the immediate presence of God down "to the tenth generation." David himself in his great and passionate heart for God, however, could never bear the thought of being excluded from the immediate presence of Jehovah. A way must be found for David to "dwell in the house of the LORD all the days of [his] life, to gaze upon the beauty of the LORD and to seek Him in His temple" (Ps. 27:4). That way would be found in the conquest of the ancient Jebusite city of Jerusalem.

In the footnotes of *The NIV Study Bible,* a comment is made concerning David's Psalm 110. "It may be...that David composed the psalm for the coronation of his son Solomon..."[7] I believe the commentator has stumbled upon something. In this messianic psalm, David declares: "The LORD has sworn and will not change his mind: 'You are a priest forever, in the order of Melchizedek'" (Ps. 110:4). According to the argument in the Book of Hebrews, Jesus' descent from the Davidic line of Judah was not a *hindrance* to His royal priesthood, but *the means* by which He entered into that royal priesthood, the priesthood of Melchizedek. "For it is clear that our Lord descended from Judah..." (Heb. 7:14). This is how that apparently came about. When David conquered the ancient city of Melchizedek, he activated by faith and took to himself that dormant priesthood of Melchizedek in order that he, as a new kind of priest, could have unhindered access to the presence of Jehovah. He then could commit that royal priesthood of Melchizedek to the generations that would spring from his loins. Eventually, one would be born from David's seed of whom *alone* it could be written that "*He lives,*" and because Jesus *lives forever,* He is able to fully walk out that royal priesthood (see Heb. 7:23-24). "Therefore He is able to save completely those who come to God through Him, because *He always lives* to intercede for them" (Heb. 7:25). Jesus now ministers as our great High Priest by "the power of an indestructible life. For it is declared: 'You are a priest forever, in the order of Melchizedek'" (Heb. 7:16-17).

David would be not only a prophet and a king but also a prophet *and a priest* and a king—a priest in the order of Melchizedek. He would not be excluded from the presence of God, nor even be satisfied with the once-yearly, limited, Day of Atonement access of the Aaronic high priests from Levi. David would have bold and unlimited access—day and night, anytime and all the time—to the presence of his best, his heavenly Friend. Behold David, the beloved of God, the man after God's own heart!

Taking a Step of Faith

Father, many are the hindrances to my own enjoyment of Your immediate presence. The ramifications of my birth, my background, and my own backslidings have blocked my pathway. But like David Your servant, I rise up in the strength of Your grace and enter in through the veil by that "new and living way" provided for me by Your son Jesus! I "draw near...with a sincere heart in full assurance of faith, having [my heart] sprinkled to cleanse [me] from a guilty conscience and having [my body] washed with pure water" (Heb. 10:22). I do take my stand this day in Your Holy of Holies presence. Amen!

Day Sixteen

Bringing Back the Ark

▶ Scripture Reading: 2 Samuel 6; 1 Chronicles 13

...Bring up...the ark of God the LORD, who is enthroned between the cherubim—the ark that is called by the Name.

1 Chronicles 13:6

We are told in First Chronicles 10:14 that Saul, son of Kish, "did not inquire of the LORD. So the LORD put him to death and turned the kingdom over to David son of Jesse." Then we are told in First Chronicles 13:3 that among the very first words of David after his coronation as king were: "Let us bring the ark of our God back to us, for we did not inquire of it [*of him*, margin] during the reign of Saul."

Where, exactly, was the ark? Where was this throne of Jehovah? The ark of God was in exile on the Philistine border of Judah, not quite ten miles west of Jerusalem in a small town called Kiriath Jearim, Baalah of Judah. Nearly a hundred years before, the ark of God in the days of Eli the priest had been captured by the Philistines. Taken initially to Ashdod, to the temple of their god Dagon, the ark would teach the Philistines something of the "terror of the Lord." As the temple doors were opened one morning for services, Dagon was found lying on his face on the ground before the ark of Jehovah. The next day he was found in the same position with his head and hands broken off! Indeed, "the LORD's hand was heavy upon the people of Ashdod and its vicinity; He brought devastation upon them and afflicted them with tumors [in the groin]" (1 Sam. 5:6; see marginal note). In desperation the Philistines moved the ark of God from Ashdod to Gath and then from Gath to Ekron. In each city a plague broke out, and the city was filled with panic until at last the ark was restored to Judean soil, carried on a Philistine cart and miraculously drawn by cows who were willing to leave their newborn calves in order to do the bidding of God! The ark of the covenant finally rested at Abinadab's house, home also of Eleazar his son, who guarded the ark, along with Uzzah and Ahio, Abinadab's grandsons, who would virtually grow up with the ark.

All through the long years of Saul's reign, the ark remained at Kiriath Jearim. It was never returned to Shiloh, where the tabernacle of Moses originally stood; nor was it ever brought to Gibeon, where the tabernacle was later erected, about eight miles northwest of Jerusalem. Saul simply had no interest in the ark of God. He had no hunger for the presence of God; he had no vision for the throne of Jehovah to be restored to the Lord's house. Saul was a man without a passion for God; he was neither hot nor lukewarm. He was cold, and for that reason he was easily turned aside to inquire at the door of the spiritualist medium of Endor; that is also why Jehovah Himself killed Saul and "turned the kingdom over to David son of Jesse" (1 Chron. 10:13-14). Saul simply had no heart to "inquire of the LORD."

But it was not so with David, the son of Jesse. His passion was for the presence of the Lord. His hunger was for the manifest glory of God. He had just dedicated Jerusalem to be the capital of Jehovah's kingdom, and now the King Himself must come and establish His throne in the midst of this holy city! David had seized and activated the priesthood of Melchizedek, ancient king of Jerusalem; now there must be a glorious King present in His temple to be worshipped, honored, and adored! So the cry went up from the heart of David:

> "Let us bring the ark of our God back to us...." So David assembled all the Israelites from the Shihor River in Egypt to Lebo Hamath [north in Syria], to bring the ark of God from Kiriath Jearim. David and all the Israelites with him went to Baalah of Judah (Kiriath Jearim) to bring up from there the ark of God the LORD, who is enthroned between the cherubim—the ark that is called by the Name (1 Chronicles 13:3, 5-6).

The Lord, perhaps with foreknowledge of a king such as David, had carefully prescribed through His servant Moses some 400 years before:

When you enter the land that the LORD your God is giving you...and you say, "Let us set a king over us like all the nations around us" ...   When he takes the throne of his kingdom, he is to write for himself on a scroll a copy of this law, taken from that of the priests, who are Levites.   It is to be with him, and *he is to read it all the days of his life so that he may learn to revere the LORD his God* and follow carefully all the words of this law and these decrees *and not consider himself better than his brothers* and turn from the law to the right or to the left... (Deuteronomy 17:14, 18-20).

This is especially important for prophetic-type souls, such as David, who might tend at times to act on the strength of their own revelations rather than according to the clearly revealed Word of God.

David, with 30,000 chosen men of Israel, went down to Baalah of Judah to recover the ark of God. We are told that "they set the ark of God on a new cart," just as the Philistines had done nearly a century before (2 Sam. 6:3). Uzzah and Ahio, who had grown up around the ark, were guiding the ark as the oxen pulled it along. David was ecstatic, leading the celebration, rejoicing with all his might with songs of praise and with instruments of thanksgiving. But at the threshing floor of Nacon the unthinkable happened. The oxen stumbled. The ark began to topple. Uzzah reached out his hand to steady the ark—and was struck dead in the presence of God!

The music stopped; the procession halted. People gathered around, looking on in utter confusion and dismay, and David became very angry. After his first flash of rage, fear filled David's heart, and "he was not willing to take the ark of the LORD to be with him in the City of David. Instead, he took it aside to the house of Obed-Edom the Gittite" (2 Sam. 6:10). There it remained for three months until David gained his bearings.

Uzzah, we are told, was struck by God because of his irreverent act. He had become so used to having the ark around that familiarity had bred contempt; he thought nothing of touching the holy ark. David had erred in this process, as he later admitted in First Chronicles 15:13, because he "did not inquire of [the LORD] about how to do it in the prescribed way." He had sought to do God's will using carnal methods, a frequent failure on the part of many both then and now.

In closing our thoughts, we might ask, "Who is Obed-Edom the Gittite?" Gittites were Philistine inhabitants from Gath. Obed-Edom was more than likely a Philistine convert, a worshipper of Jehovah. The ark remained in his home for three months, during which time the Lord blessed his household and everything he had. Obed-Edom will be mentioned again and again in the sacred record (see 1 Chron. 13:13-14; 15:18,21,24; 26:4-5,8,15), where he appears as a sort of Levite, but without a Levitical genealogy. Obed-Edom the Gittite and his sons for generations after him will serve as Levites in the house of

the Lord under David's direction—perhaps in a preview of
Jehovah's ultimate intent to draw into the new
commonwealth of Israel many who, apart from His grace,
would otherwise continue to be aliens, strangers, and
foreigners to His eternal purpose. God blessed Obed-Edom,
and of one thing I am sure: As David heard of how the
Lord blessed Obed-Edom's home, everyone in it, and
everything he possessed, he thought again of how he
himself needed that very closeness of the presence of his
God. "Now King David was told, 'The LORD has blessed
the household of Obed-Edom and everything he has,
because of the ark of God.'" As a result "David went down
and brought up the ark of God from the house of Obed-
Edom to the City of David with rejoicing" (2 Sam. 6:12).
Such is David, son of Jesse—a man who can never be
content without the abiding sense of the nearness of
Jehovah, the closeness of his God.

Taking a Step of Faith

*Spirit of the Living God, You are the kindler of the fire
of God within my bosom; You are the source of my passion
for Jesus. Apart from Your presence and Your working
within my soul, I am cold and lifeless. Come, kindle Your
flame within my heart! Give me a passion for the presence
of my God. Give me the same kind of heart that You gave
Your servant David! For Jesus' sake, I pray. Amen.*

Day Seventeen

The Simple Tent of David

▶ Scripture Reading: 1 Chronicles 15 and 16

I will allow no sleep to my eyes, no slumber to my eyelids, till I find a place for the LORD, a dwelling for the Mighty One of Jacob.
David's promise in Psalm 132:4-5

Three times in the beginning of First Chronicles 15, we are told that David "prepared a place" on Mount Zion, in the City of David, for the ark of God (1 Chron. 15:1,3,12). It was a humble place that David prepared—a simple *tent*—but it was right in David's own backyard, if you will! With jubilation and with rejoicing David brought up the ark of God from the house of Obed-Edom, carried with poles on the shoulders of the Levites, "as Moses had commanded in accordance with the word of the LORD" (1 Chron. 15:15). Thus the ark wended its way over the remaining few miles to Jerusalem, the city of God!

It is in conjunction with the bringing up of the ark that we first notice the priestly doings of David. "Now David was clothed in a robe of fine linen, *as were all the Levites* who were carrying the ark...and Kenaniah, who was in charge of the singing of the choirs. *David also wore a linen ephod*" (1 Chron. 15:27). These garments—the linen robe and the linen ephod—were *priestly* garments, as the New International Version footnote tells us. David was dressed as a priest of God Most High, a priest after the order of Melchizedek, if you will.

When the ark of God finally arrived in the City of David, they "set it inside the tent that David had pitched for it," and we are then told that "after David had finished *sacrificing the burnt offerings and fellowship offerings he blessed the people in the name of the LORD*" (1 Chron. 16:1-2). We will yet be informed by Ezra, the chronicler, in First Chronicles 23:13, that these very functions were all priestly functions: "to consecrate the most holy things, *to offer sacrifices before the LORD*, to minister before Him and *to pronounce blessings in His name forever*." David performed these very functions as part of his priestly ministry.

David's sole purpose in placing the ark of God in the simple tent (which he called "the temple") in his own backyard, rather than returning it to its place in the tabernacle of Moses at Gibeon, is revealed more fully for us in David's Psalm 27. Hear his words:

> One thing I have asked from the LORD, that I shall
> seek: that I may dwell in the house of the LORD
> all the days of my life, to behold the beauty of the
> LORD, and to meditate [literally, *inquire*] in His

temple. For in the day of trouble He will conceal me in His tabernacle; in the secret place of His tent He will hide me; He will lift me up on a rock. ...and I will offer in His tent sacrifices with shouts of joy; I will sing, yes, I will sing praises to the LORD (Psalm 27:4-6 NASB).

Here is a man enjoying more of an intimate closeness to the ark of God and to the glorious Shekinah presence of God Himself than any Aaronic high priest ever could in his once-a-year, Day of Atonement gingerly visit to the Holy of Holies in the tabernacle of Moses. Here is David, a priest after the order of Melchizedek, pressing close to the very heart of Israel's God.

It would be here, in the unveiled presence of God, that the inner healing David so sorely needed would continue to take place, for David goes on in Psalm 27 to explore some of his own personal pain:

Hear, O LORD, when I cry with my voice, and be gracious to me and answer me. When Thou didst say, 'Seek My face,' my heart said to Thee, 'Thy face, O LORD I shall seek.' *Do not hide Thy face from me, do not turn Thy servant away in anger...do not abandon me nor forsake me.... For my father and my mother have forsaken me, but the LORD will take me up* (Psalm 27:7-10 NASB).

Much of the emotional brokenness in David's life was related, I believe, to a deep sense of abandonment that David carried in his heart even from the days of his youth.

His fear of Jehovah's rejecting him, turning away from him, and forsaking him was clearly related, according to this psalm, to the abandonment he felt from his father Jesse and from his mother (possibly for the reasons we have touched on). But as David sat in the healing presence of the Lord, gazing on His awesome beauty, he came to understand that "*the LORD will take me up*" (KJV); He will "welcome and comfort me" (TLB).

Some years ago, I gingerly began to seek the Lord's face concerning my own inner emotional brokenness. As I sat before the Lord, bathed in His presence, I uncovered within my own heart a deep sense of personal abandonment. I saw that I had deep insecurities in my life—insecurities that were at the root of why I possessively clutched various relationships in such unhealthy ways, even to the point of sin. I feared that if I somehow let go, I would find myself abandoned and alone—again. In a revelation from the Lord, I was able to trace that deep sense of abandonment back to my childhood. I saw myself as a little boy lying on my bed paralyzed with anxiety. My concerned mother, fearing the rages of her alcoholic husband, would flee the house in the midnight hours, leaving me helplessly alone, locked in my bedroom until the next morning. It was only many years later as a grown man that I learned my mother was able to go to the home of a close Christian friend to stay the night until my father was sobered up. But in my boyhood years, all I could think of was that my mother was walking the treacherous streets of Brooklyn, New York, alone in the dark hours of the night. Many times I wondered if I would ever see her alive again. As I sat in the Lord's presence, that deep sense of abandonment was uncovered in my heart. But also uncovered in my heart was a new-born assurance that "*the LORD will take me up*," He will "welcome and comfort *me*." And so the healing process began! Praise God!

As we draw our thoughts about David's new-found priesthood to a conclusion, it is interesting for me to note the statement in 2 Samuel 8:18 concerning David's court appointments: "and David's sons were *royal advisers*." The New International Version margin simply reads that they "were *priests*." The Hebrew word that the New International Version translates as "royal advisers" is *kohen*. It appears 730 times in the Hebrew Scriptures and is translated 729 of those times in the New International Version as "priests." Only this one time—here—is this word *kohen* translated as "royal advisers." (At least the New International Version was bold enough to put it correctly in the margin!) The fact is that David's sons were appointed by him as *priests*, and so more than likely Psalm 110 *was* written for Solomon, his appointed successor: "*You are a priest* forever, in the order of Melchizedek." There remains no doubt in my own mind that David was prophet *and priest* and king, a foreshadowing of his great messianic son, our Lord Jesus. Never was there a priest like David, and never was there a worship center quite like David's simple tabernacle on Mount Zion! David appointed singers and players of numerous instruments and whole choirs to worship before the Lord "continually" (see 1 Chron. 15:16, 27; 16:6 KJV). David, on that very first day, personally wrote a medley of praise for them to sing—verses that would become for us parts of Psalms 96, 105, and 106. The tabernacle of David was indeed a royal house of worship—spontaneous, prophetic, anointed worship—and a place of adoration, thanksgiving, and praise!

> Look to the LORD and His strength; seek His face always. ... Splendor and majesty are before Him; strength and joy in His dwelling place. ... Bring an offering and come before Him; worship the LORD in the splendor of His holiness. ... Give thanks to the LORD, for He is good; His [covenant] love endures forever. ... Praise be to the LORD, the God of Israel, from everlasting to everlasting (1 Chronicles 16:11,27,29,34,36).

It is little wonder, then, that the Lord would speak a stunning end-time promise through his prophet Amos: "In that day I will raise up the tabernacle of David that is fallen...I will build it as in the days of old" (Amos 9:11 KJV). It is little wonder that the best definition that James, the half-brother of our Lord Jesus, could give to the apostolic church was that it, the church, was simply an expression of that promised restoration spoken of by Amos: the restoration of the tabernacle of David (see Acts 15:12-18)! This is what our God has always wanted His people to be: a demonstration of the anointed, spontaneous, prophetic worship and praise that David moved in. This is what God will restore again at the end of this age: the glorious phenomenon known as "David's tabernacle," rebuilt and restored, so "that the remnant of men may seek the Lord, and all the Gentiles who bear My name, says the Lord, who does these things" (Acts 15:17). Amen!

Taking a Step of Faith

*Gracious Father, I draw near to You. Shine the spotlight of Your Holy Spirit into my heart. Uncover my broken places; reveal the shattered state of my own heart—my insecurities, my fear of abandonment, my pain. Bring to bear upon my soul Your cleansing, restoring grace. Cause me to know, by Your Spirit, that You will **never** leave me, nor will You ever forsake me. I believe that You will heal me deep within, and I believe that this healing will begin today. I believe that You will bring me into a fresh place of spontaneous, anointed, prophetic praise and worship, as a royal priest in the order of Melchizedek! In the name of Jesus, I come. Amen.*

Day Eighteen

A Different Kind of Leadership

▶ Scripture Reading: 1 Chronicles 11:10-12:38

And David shepherded them with integrity of heart; with skillful hands he led them.

Psalm 78:72

Between the account of David's coronation as king over all Israel and the account of David's bringing back the ark of God to Jerusalem, Ezra inserts into the sacred record some very revealing insights into the leadership style of David. His was a different kind of leadership in comparison to Saul's, and surely new in comparison to the prevailing leadership styles of the surrounding empires of his day.

1. David's *pursuit of the Lord* has already been etched upon our hearts and minds from the sacred account. Saul died because he "did not inquire of the LORD," but David was a man in pursuit of God. David required God's presence with him, for David knew that the success of his leadership depended upon the presence of God with him.

123

So it was that "David became more and more powerful, *because* the LORD Almighty [Jehovah of Hosts] was with him" (1 Chron. 11:9). Our leadership in our homes, in our workplaces, and in God's Kingdom is absolutely linked to the presence of the Lord with us. My wife and my children should be able to break in upon me at any time and find me waiting on God in prayer or pouring over the Scriptures, seeking God's face. They have a right to know that I am a man in pursuit of God, as do my coworkers and my fellow members in the Body of Christ. The essence of all good leadership is that it is godly, and that means that a man or a woman is in pursuit of *God*.

2. David's *passionate purpose* in the exercise of his leadership was "for the LORD." The kingdom was the Lord's; the throne was the "throne of the LORD"; the people were the people *of God*. Everything was *for Him*. I believe one of the most challenging statements I have ever read is one by Watchman Nee: *"I want nothing for myself; I want everything for the Lord."*[8] In First Chronicles 11:15-19 we have the account of the three who broke through the Philistine lines and procured water from the well near the gate of Bethlehem because they knew David longed for this water. The touching response of David to their sacrifice was that "he refused to drink it; instead, he poured it out before [literally, *to*] the LORD." David wanted nothing for himself, but everything for the Lord. This passionate purpose is at the heart of all great leadership. Spiritually sensitive men and women will follow this kind of leadership.

3. David's *proper positioning* of others showed his wisdom in recognizing and utilizing the skills of those whom he was leading. First Chronicles 11:10-47, which is a listing of "David's mighty men...[who] gave his kingship strong support," is a fascinating study in this art of proper positioning. Mention is made of "the Thirty" and of "the Three" and of "Abishai, the brother of Joab [who] was *chief* of the Three," who "became as famous as the Three. ...even though he was not included among them [the Three]." Sometimes the language becomes so involved that even the commentators cannot figure it out, but one thing is certain: David recognized and utilized the individual skills of his mighty men, and he positioned them according to their graces and gifts.

In our congregation we have *daily* leadership interaction, a *weekly* planning meeting with a wider circle of leadership, a *monthly* evening pastoral staff meeting with a yet wider circle of leadership, and a *quarterly* Saturday breakfast with over 120 men and women who are in the widest circle of leadership in our church. In this way, we seek to walk in the steps of our kingdom-mentor David. He was skillful in his leadership in Jehovah's kingdom, and we must seek the Lord for similar skills so that, as a result of our leadership, every member of Christ's Body will be properly utilized to the maximum and that all might receive their "well done" at His appearing.

4. David's ability to *empower others* to serve, as well as his grace in *receiving empowerment* from others, is a further key aspect of his skills in leadership. First

Chronicles 12 is a study in David's ability to empower others. A number of those who came to David at Ziklag were Benjamites, kinsmen of Saul (see 1 Chron. 12:2-7,16-18). Initially, David very honestly expressed his concerns about them; there was the possibility they could eventually betray him to Saul, who himself was a Benjamite. But notwithstanding his cautions, David took that leap of faith and "received them and *made them leaders* of his raiding bands" (1 Chron. 12:18). Many times in our leadership of others we are called upon to take a similar leap of faith—to trust and to utilize those who may not yet have totally proven themselves. Yet in that very trust and utilization we actually empower them to fulfill their calling. On the other hand, we can be so insecure and cautious in our leadership that our mistrust only cripples the very people we are seeking to bring forth into their place in the Kingdom. David's skills are a challenge to us.

In the midst of this interaction with the Benjamites, David himself is prophetically affirmed and empowered in his own leadership. "Then the Spirit came upon Amasai, chief of the Thirty, and he said: 'We are yours, O David! We are with you, O son of Jesse! Success, success to you, and success to those who help you, for your God will help you'" (1 Chron. 12:18). Happy is the Christian who is a part of such an affirming, empowering body of believers. Blessed is the pastoral staff—men and women—who are being prophetically affirmed and empowered by those whom they are seeking to serve. Only in this way is the best brought out in all of us.

5. Finally, David understood the wise leadership principle of encouraging *wide participation in the decision-making process.* It is a poor leadership skill for one or for a few to make critical decisions *for* a whole group and then expect that whole group to walk out those decisions. Wise leadership seeks to involve everyone's participation in the decision-making process, for when people have helped to decide a course of action, they have a personal investment in that course of action and will give themselves more wholeheartedly to its outworking and accomplishment.

At his coronation banquet (which may have involved up to one-third of a million people), David did an unusual thing. Contrary to the autocratic and despotic leadership modes of the kings and pharaohs who surrounded him, "David conferred with *each* of his officers, the commanders of thousands and commanders of hundreds. He then said to *the whole assembly* of Israel, '*If it seems good to you* and if it is the will of the LORD our God.... Let us bring the ark of our God back to us'" (1 Chron. 13:1-3). Here was a man who asked for the participation of everyone in the decision-making process; here was a man who believed that the whole congregation could hear from God and could thereby help to discern the will of God. As a result of being involved in the decision-making process, "the whole assembly agreed to do this, because *it seemed right to all the people*" (1 Chron. 13:4). So it was that "David *and all the Israelites with him* went to Baalah of Judah (Kiriath Jearim) to bring up from there the ark of God the LORD..." (1 Chron. 13:6).

The ecclesiastical question always on the table concerns what form of church government is the correct one. If we learn anything from David's leadership, we learn that Jehovah's Kingdom is a *theocratic democracy*. It is said of all the people of God—not just of one or of a few—that "*we* have the mind of Christ" (1 Cor. 2:16). All the people of God are to hear from Him. Wise leadership does not subvert that from happening, but rather seeks to facilitate it. When a whole assembly is discerning God's will, they will all be there, with all their might, to carry it out!

The pharaohs of Egypt may have ruled as despots. The kings of the Arameans may have been autocrats, but the Kingdom of God is a theocratic democracy. And David's leadership existed to enhance Jehovah's headship over *all His people*.

Taking a Step of Faith

*Father, as You have called me to lead in my home, in the civic affairs of my community, in my workplace, and in Your Kingdom, I ask for divine skill in that leading. Give me a heart that pursues You. Give me that passionate purpose in order that everything will be **for You**; give me wisdom in properly positioning and empowering others; and deliver me from those insecurities within me that tend to make me autocratic and despotic. Deliver me from heavy-handedness. Give me a heart to see all Your people raised up before You. Give me a vision to see all Your people hearing from You and obeying You and discovering and fulfilling their calling. For Jesus' sake. Amen.*

Day Nineteen

No Longer a Victim

▸ Scripture Reading: 1 Chronicles 17

I have made a covenant with My chosen one, I have sworn to David My servant, "I will establish your line forever and make your throne firm through all generations."

Psalm 89:3-4

David's heart was restless. He was well settled in his royal palace which Hiram the King of Tyre had built for him (see 1 Chron. 14:1), but David's heart was still unsettled. His anguish was reflected in his words to Nathan the prophet: "Here I am, living in a palace of cedar, while the ark of the covenant of the LORD is under a tent" (1 Chron. 17:1)! Nathan's best advice to David was, "Whatever you have in mind, do it, for God is with you," but Nathan's best advice was wrong. "Go and tell my servant David...'You are not the one to build Me a house to dwell in...'" the Lord declared (1 Chron. 17:2-4). Furthermore the Lord said He would "build a house *for you*" (1 Chron. 17:10)! So First Chronicles 17 becomes a high water mark in the Holy Scriptures, for here the high and lofty One Himself steps down from eternity to make an everlasting covenant with his chosen David. That covenant, in turn, becomes the very foundation of the new covenant given to us through our Lord Jesus Christ. Hear Jehovah as He cries out to His people through Isaiah the prophet: "Give ear and come to Me; hear Me, that your soul may live. I will make an *everlasting* covenant with you, My faithful [covenant] love promised to David" (Is. 55:3).

Yes, David had a passion to build a temporal house for Jehovah, but Jehovah had an even greater passion to build a "forever" house for David—an eternal dynasty, a line that would begin with David's immediate successor and culminate in the royal seed of the eternal Christ! Jehovah promised, "I will establish his throne *forever*. I will be his father, and he will be My son. I will never take My [covenant] love away from him.... I will set him over My house and My kingdom *forever*; his throne will be established *forever*" (1 Chron. 17:12-14). Eight times in this revelation Jehovah used the word *forever*—a word that can refer only to the reign of our everlasting Lord!

When Nathan delivered this awesome revelation to him, David was overwhelmed. He simply "went in and sat before the LORD," gazing upon the splendor of Jehovah's glory radiating from between the cherubim (1 Chron. 17:16). Finally, David spoke three initial words to the Lord: "*Who am I?*" These three words form one of the most important questions a man or woman can ask. They are exceeded only by the words "Who are You?" when addressed to the Lord. Of primary importance is the revelation of who He Himself is. But next only to that revelation of who He is must come the revelation of "*who I am.*" We need to know exactly who we are!

At this juncture in his dialogue with Jehovah, David made a most powerful observation, almost in answer to his own question of "Who am I?" David exclaimed, "You have looked on me as though I were the most exalted of men, O LORD God" (1 Chron. 17:17). A closer examination of the Hebrew text reveals that these words literally read: "You...have seen me as a type of the Man who is on high, O Jehovah God" (see *Young's Literal Translation of the Holy Bible*[9] and *The Interlinear Hebrew/Greek English Bible*[10]). David, possibly for the first time, saw himself as God saw him—as a type, a picture, an imprint of "the Man who is on high"! David saw himself as the Father saw him--a man in the likeness of our Lord Jesus Christ. The Father had seen Jesus in David!

We can reasonably conclude that David began, perhaps for the first time in his life, to see himself as no longer a victim. True, he had been victimized by a generational curse and probably by an illegitimate birth; he was a victim of his parents' abandonment and of his brothers' rejection. He was a victim in the loss of his hero Saul, in the loss of his loving wife Michal, and in the loss of his closest friend Jonathan. For seven years he was the innocent victim of Saul's insane jealousy. He had also been victimized by Doeg the Edomite, and at Ziklag by the very men he sought to lead, and at Keilah by the very men he sought to serve, and by the Ziphites. All his life David had been a victim—taken advantage of, abandoned, abused, betrayed. But on this covenant day, I believe, David began to stop being a victim and started to become a victor. O Lord, "You have seen me as...the Man who is on high"! "You see me as You see Your Son! When You see me, You see Him!" There must come a day for every one of us also, a covenant day, when we too shed the skin of our own victim mentality and step into that victorious life of who Christ is in us and who we are in Him! On that glad day we shall no longer continue to be victims; rather we shall begin to become victors—more than conquerors through Him who loved us. On that day we will no longer allow ourselves to be tormented by the thought of things done to us by others; we will glory in the thought of what He has done for us! No longer will we allow ourselves to be in turmoil over how others see us; instead we will rest in the grand revelation of how He sees us—the apple of His eye, His beloved, His very own child loved with an everlasting love!

The very next words of David in First Chronicles 17:18-19 are fascinating. Kenneth Taylor in The Living Bible sees something in the Hebrew text that causes him to write this passage as "What else can I say? You know that I am *but a dog*, yet You have decided to honor me!" The Jerusalem Bible picks up the same inference in its translation: "For Your servant's sake, *this dog of Yours*, You have done such a great thing by revealing all this greatness to come." I believe it is a balancing thought. How many of the sons of God have gone over the edge in arrogance at the revelation of who they are in Christ and at the thought of who He is in them! I understand that the man who later became the self-styled "Father Divine," starting down his pride-filled path to destruction by declaring himself to be God, began it all with a legitimate revelation of "Christ in you, the hope of glory" (Col. 1:27). What, then, shall keep *my* feet from stumbling? Just the further revelation that in and of myself I am not much more than "*a dog*"—"*this dog of Yours.*" When we clearly see the counterbalancing revelation of how utterly worthless we are in and of ourselves, we can then *safely* glory in who we are in Christ!

David ended these considerations with the exclamation, "There is no one like You, O LORD...!" (1 Chron. 17:20). I smiled to myself as I read these words. Jehovah had, in effect, been saying to David, "There is no one like you, David," and now David exclaimed to Jehovah, "There is no one like You, O LORD...!" Here are two beings very much in love with each other—Jehovah and David—and they are now bound together forever in a covenant of love! Indeed, "...I have made a covenant with My chosen one, I have sworn to David my servant" (Ps. 89:3). "...If you can break My covenant with the day and My covenant with the night, so that day and night no longer come at their appointed time, then My covenant with David My servant...can be broken..." (Jer. 33:20-21).

Taking a Step of Faith

*Father, too long have I allowed myself to remain a victim. You know full well the abuses in my life; the pain and the fracturing of my inner being. You were there at my conception and at my birth; You were there during my childhood and during those abusive, hurtful, and humiliating experiences as I was growing up; and You know all too well the pain inflicted on me even by Your Church. Forgive me for allowing my life to continue to be overshadowed and molded by those hurtful experiences. **I will no longer remain a victim!** This very hour I do take the place You have provided for me **in your Son.** I thank You that You have placed me inside of Him, and that You have placed Him inside of me! I thank You that You now see me as You see Him! I thank You that You love me and that You give me this day Your everlasting covenant, Your "faithful covenant love promised to David." I thank You, Father, in Jesus' precious name! Amen!*

Day Twenty

Success in Spiritual Warfare

▶ Scripture Reading: 1 Chronicles 18 and 19

Praise be to the LORD my Rock, who trains my hands for war, my fingers for battle.

Psalm 144:1

It should not surprise us that Ezra the chronicler followed the powerful account of God's covenant love for David and of David's realization of who he was in Christ in First Chronicles 17 with the account of David's military triumphs in First Chronicles 18 and 19. It is out of these twin revelations of how loved we are in our Lord Jesus and of how powerful He is in us that we are then able to take our place as "more than conquerors through Him who loved us. ...convinced that neither death nor life, neither angels nor demons, neither the present nor the future, nor any powers, neither height nor depth, nor anything else in all creation, will be able to separate us from the love of God that is in Christ Jesus our Lord" (Rom. 8:37-39).

David was a brilliant military genius and an inspiring empire builder. We have already noted that under Saul the kingdom had dwindled. Saul in all of his battles had lost more ground to the Philistines than he had gained; the kingdom was smaller at his death than when he first became king. It was David who extended the perimeters of the kingdom and made Israel one of the most powerful empires of his day, reaching in the south from the Red Sea on the borders of Egypt to the Euphrates River in the far north. For the first time in Israel's history, the commission given to Joshua by Jehovah in Joshua 1:3-5 had been fulfilled! First Chronicles 18 and 19 give us some of the grand details of this.

David's conquests extended to the west, to the east, to the north, and to the south of the kingdom of Israel. On the western front, "...David defeated the Philistines and subdued them, and he took Gath and its surrounding villages from the control of the Philistines" (1 Chron. 18:1). First Chronicles 14 had already given us a more detailed account of this conquest of the Philistines. Ezra was impressed to move the account of David's military campaigns against the Philistines forward in his chronicle to illustrate the passion of David's heart in bringing back the ark of God so that he and Israel might *inquire of Jehovah* (see 1 Chron. 13:3)—something Saul and Israel had failed to do during his reign. Twice in chapter 14, David's victory over the Philistines was directly attributed to the fact that "David inquired of God" (14:9) and "David inquired of God again, and God answered him..." (14:14). Thus, not because of well-formed human plans, but because of divine strategies, the Philistines were defeated and 60 years of Philistine invasion and occupation were broken. In this western campaign, we also take special note that as the Philistine armies fled, they "abandoned their gods...and David gave orders to burn them in the fire" (14:12). Here we touch on the first of the three strategic goals of David's military campaigns: *to expand the borders of Jehovah's reign; to see the kingdoms of this world, in some small measure, become the kingdom of our Lord and of His Christ!* David burned the demon gods of the Philistines in the fire, and perhaps men like Obed-Edom the Gittite, the Philistine convert of First Chronicles 13:13-14, became typical of the spiritual spoils that David gained by these conquests.

Later, in the eastern campaign against the Ammonites at the city of Rabbah, we are told in Second Samuel 12:30 that David "took the crown from the head of their king [margin, *Milcom*, that is, Molech]—its weight was a talent of gold, and it was set with precious stones—and it was placed on David's head...." The crown weighed a talent (between 75 and 80 pounds)—too heavy for a human monarch to consistently wear. The ancient manuscripts stating that the crown was taken "from the head of *Milcom*" are undoubtedly correct. The crown apparently sat on the head of the idol Milcom (that is, Molech), the chief demon god of the Ammonites. According to Jewish tradition, the brazen image of Molech was hollowed out as a fire pot. Its face was the face of a calf, with arms outstretched to receive the babies who were put into its hands as human sacrifices offered to appease this firegod, the lord of the

Ammonites. In the subjugation of the Ammonite kingdom to the Lord, Molech's crown was placed, ever so briefly, on David's head as Jehovah's representative, declaring that Jehovah was indeed the sovereign King of all kings and Lord over all lords!

Repeatedly in his conquests, David declared this to be his prime strategy: he wanted the land to be "subject to *the LORD* and to His people" (1 Chron. 22:18). Indeed, the throne of Israel was "the throne of the kingdom of *the LORD*" (1 Chron. 28:5), for "everything in heaven and earth is *Yours. Yours*, O LORD, is the kingdom; *You* are exalted as head over all. ...*You* are the ruler of all things..." (1 Chron. 29:11-12). So the expanding throne of David became the expanding "throne of *the LORD*" (1 Chron. 29:23)! David writes in Psalm 86:8-10: "Among the gods there is none like You, O Lord; no deeds can compare with Yours. All the nations You have made will come and worship before You, O Lord; they will bring glory to Your name. For You are great and do marvelous deeds; You alone are God." Indeed, the primary purpose in David's spiritual warfare (as it is in ours today) is the extension of the borders of Jehovah's reign, that men and women everywhere might come to "repentance leading them to a knowledge of the truth, and that they will come to their senses and escape from the trap of the devil, who has taken them captive to do his will" (2 Tim. 2:25-26).

The campaign to the east against Moab is briefly described in First Chronicles 18:2: "David also defeated the Moabites, and they became subject to him and *brought tribute.*" Second Samuel 8:2 describes in more detail the bloody vengeance David heaped upon the Moabites. Bearing in mind David's own Moabite blood and the fact that about twenty years ago he had also left his own mother and father in the hands of the king of Moab for safekeeping (see 1 Sam. 22:3-4), we are left puzzled at David's extreme cruelty against the Moabites. There is a Jewish tradition that tells us that David used this severity with the Moabites because they had slain his parents and brethren, whom he put under the protection of the King of Moab during his exile. Perhaps in the dance of these grievous circumstances, David became the initial fulfillment of Balaam's messianic prophecy of some 400 years before: "I see him, but not now; I behold him, but not near. A star will come out of Jacob; a scepter will rise out of Israel. *He will crush the foreheads of Moab*, the skulls of all the sons of Sheth" (Num. 24:17).

The northern campaign against the Arameans (recorded in First Chronicles 18:3-10 and then amplified in chapter 19) also *brought much tribute to David*, as did the campaign against Moab.

> David took the gold shields carried by the officers of Hadadezer [king of Zobah, one of the Aramean states] and brought them to Jerusalem. From Tebah and Cun, towns that belonged to Hadadezer, David took a great quantity of bronze, which Solomon used to make the bronze Sea, the pillars and various bronze articles (1 Chronicles 18:7-8).

Tou, King of Hamath, a chief city in upper Syria in the Orontes valley, also sent to David a tribute of gratitude for the defeat of his enemy Hadadezer: "...all kinds of articles of gold and silver and bronze. King David dedicated these articles to the LORD, as he had done with the silver and gold he had taken from...Edom and Moab, the Ammonites and the Philistines, and Amalek" (1 Chron. 18:10-11).

This vast wealth accumulated in plunder and tribute brings to light the second of David's strategic goals in his military campaigns: *to pour into the treasury of Jehovah the wealth needed to build a magnificent house for Jehovah's excellent glory!* Over the next nearly twenty years of his life, David would gather "a hundred thousand talents [3,750 tons] of gold" and "a million talents [37,500 tons] of silver" and "quantities of bronze and iron too great to be weighed, and wood and stone..." (1 Chron. 22:14). The value of these building materials in our modern currency is well over 50 billion dollars! All of this, as the spoils of war, David dedicated to build the temple of the Lord!

David's third strategic goal in his military campaigns was simply *to secure the borders of Israel* in fulfillment of the Lord's covenant word to him: "...I have cut off all your enemies from before you. ... And I will provide a place for My people Israel and will plant them so that they can have a home of their own and no longer be disturbed..." (1 Chron. 17:8-9). And so the Lord granted His people rest on every side (see 1 Chron. 22:18), for "the LORD gave David victory everywhere he went" (1 Chron. 18:13).

Taking a Step of Faith

*Lord of the armies of Heaven, You have called me to spiritual warfare—to stand in the strength of Your might against rulers, against authorities, against the powers of this dark world, and against spiritual forces of evil in the heavenly realms. I take my stand this day **to see Your Kingdom extended into the lives of men and women** who all their lives have been held as captives of satan. I also take my stand this day **to see Your glorious Temple built**—constructed out of the spoils of this warfare, from the living stones of the men and women You are redeeming. I also take my stand this day **to see the spiritual borders of my home, my work, my neighborhood, and my church secured in peace**, safe from the attacks of the evil one. I take my stand this day in Your very own Son. I clothe myself, by faith, with Christ, my spiritual armor!*

I receive Your girding truth, Lord Jesus, as my belt, and Your protective righteousness as my breastplate. I put on the shoes of readiness that come from Your good news of peace. I take up Your all-encompassing shield of faith, the very faith of the Son of God. I place the helmet of Your everlasting salvation on my head, and I take up the weapons of Your eternal Spirit—Your living Word—to be in my mouth as a sharp, double-edged sword! Prevail in prayer through me this day, O great ever-interceding Melchizedek, on every occasion and for every saint. I pray in Your dear name. Amen.

Day Twenty-one

When Kings and Priests Stumble and Fall

▶ Scripture Reading: 2 Samuel 11 and 12

In the spring, at the time when kings go off to war...David remained in Jerusalem...

1 Chronicles 20:1

David's adultery with Bathsheba was not a teenager's indiscriminate fling; it was a grown man's midlife crisis. It seems as if David was fully 50 years old when First Chronicles 20:1 records: "In the spring, at the time when kings go off to war...David remained in Jerusalem..." As a matter of fact, this occurred in the midst of the great eastern campaign against the Ammonite kingdom and against the armies of the Aramean states (whom Hanun, King of the Ammonites, had hired to protect his borders; cf. 1 Chron. 19). Ezra, in First Chronicles 20, recorded nothing more than the above colorless facts for reasons that we will yet uncover.

We must turn to the original court records commissioned by David himself, and in particular the record found in Second Samuel 11 and 12, for the heartrending details of the sin that took place in that spring of 1035 B.C.

How I wish with all my heart that we could place these grievous events in David's life—his adultery with Bathsheba and his consequent murder of Uriah, her husband—*before* First Chronicles 13–17! Why did this evil not happen in David's life *before* David returned the ark of Jehovah's presence to Jerusalem, *before* he recovered Melchizedek's royal priesthood, *before* Jehovah revealed His great covenant to David, and *before* David's revelation of who he was in "the Man from above"? How can we explain such great failures *after* such great revelations? Perhaps that is part of the hidden nature of the "mystery of iniquity." And if I can understand why similar things have happened in my own life, then perhaps I can understand why they happened in David's. I believe it boils down to one issue: I cannot ever mistake revelation for experience. What has been seen by revelation must be painstakingly walked out in daily experience. It is not enough for me to seek and to cherish the presence of God; His presence must deliver me. It is not enough for me to have a revelation of Jehovah's covenant love; that love must build again the broken places deep within my life. It is not enough for me to see who I am in Him; I must experience the actual transformation of my life as I experience who He is in me. Revelation must be fleshed out in actual human experience or it leaves me experientially as not much more than an enlightened pagan.

In the scenario outlined for us in Second Samuel 11 and 12, David set himself up. He did not blindly fall into sin; he walked into it with his eyes wide open. One warm spring evening, unable to sleep, pacing back and forth on his palace roof, David saw a beautiful woman bathing in the heat of the night on the veranda of her home downhill from the royal palace. When David inquired about her, he learned of her name and her family and that *she was another man's wife*; "...Bathsheba, the daughter of Eliam and *the wife of Uriah the Hittite*" (2 Sam. 11:3). Instead of realizing "sin is crouching at your door; it desires to have you, but you must master it" (Gen. 4:7), David rushed headlong into the satisfaction of his own lusts. He sent messengers, he took Bathsheba, he lay with her, and she conceived. David then sought to cover the matter up and, in desperation, finally plotted the death of Uriah, her husband, and one of David's most loyal warriors. With Uriah dead, pierced through by Ammonite arrows at the entrance of the city of Rabbah, David could then put on a charade of great benevolence. He could take Uriah's poor widow into his home and magnanimously provide for her by taking her as his own wife!

It was the perfect cover-up. Everything seemingly went exactly as planned. David pulled it off without a hitch. "But the thing that David had done was evil in the sight of the LORD" (2 Sam. 11:27b NASB).

The Holy Spirit admonishes us through the pen of James, our Lord's brother, "Let no one say when he is tempted, 'I am being tempted by God'.... But each one is tempted when he is carried away and enticed by his own lust. Then when lust has conceived, it gives birth to sin; and when sin is accomplished, it brings forth death" (Jas. 1:13-15 NASB). I suspect that James had David in mind when he wrote those words. For nearly nine months, with the child growing inside of Bathsheba, things outwardly appeared to be going smoothly. The deception seemed complete. In Psalm 32:3-4, however, David pictured some of his own inner turmoil during those long summer months: "When I kept silent about my sin, my body wasted away through my groaning all day long. For day and night Thy hand was heavy upon me; my vitality was drained away as with the fever-heat of summer" (NASB). Then one day the proverbial shoe finally fell: "The LORD sent Nathan to David" (2 Sam. 12:1a).

Nathan came seemingly to inquire about a matter of justice in the realm. "David burned with anger" (2 Sam. 12:5a), we are told, at Nathan's account of a certain heartless man who had great flocks and herds of his own, but who stole the one little ewe lamb from his poor neighbor, the only lamb the poor man had. David's judgment was swift and clear: "As the LORD lives, surely the man who has done this deserves to die" (2 Sam. 12:5b NASB). F.B. Meyer in his biographical study, *David: Shepherd, Psalmist, King*, comments at this juncture, "We often excuse ourselves from avenging our own sin by our harsh behavior and uncharitable judgment toward others."[11] What a shock when Nathan then extended his arm and pointed his finger at David and declared *"You are the man!"* Nathan then continued to prophesy the word of the Lord, "Why have you despised the word of the LORD by doing evil in His sight? You have struck down Uriah the Hittite with the sword, have taken his wife to be your wife, and have killed him with the sword of the sons of Ammon. Now therefore, the sword shall never depart from your house because *you have despised Me*..." (2 Sam. 12:9-10 NASB).

David's immediate response was to fall at Nathan's feet in a crumpled, sobbing heap, declaring, "I have sinned against the LORD." In Psalm 32:5, we read David's full statement: "I acknowledged my sin to Thee, and my iniquity I did not hide; I said, 'I will confess my transgressions to the LORD;' and Thou didst forgive the guilt of my sin" (NASB).

Psalm 51 ("A Psalm of David, when Nathan the prophet came to him, after he had gone in to Bathsheba") contains a fuller account of David's cries of anguish before the Lord:

> I know my transgressions, and my sin is ever before me. Against Thee, Thee only, I have sinned, and done what is evil in Thy sight.... Purify me with hyssop [as a leper in Israel was purified; a leper who was otherwise incurable except for a miracle], and I shall be clean; wash me, and I shall be whiter than snow (Psalm 51:3-4,7 NASB).

Then David cried out in faith for revelation to become transformation:

Create in me a clean heart, O God, and renew a steadfast spirit within me. *[Great Creator, become my re-Creator]* Do not cast me away from Thy presence, and do not take Thy Holy Spirit from me. Restore to me the joy of Thy salvation.... The sacrifices of God are a broken spirit; a broken and a contrite heart, O God, Thou wilt not despise (Psalm 51:10-12,17 NASB).

The Lord *did* meet David on that day of deep brokenness and repentance. David recounted for us the joy of that day: "How blessed is he whose transgression is forgiven, whose sin is covered! How blessed is the man to whom the LORD does not impute iniquity, and in whose [redeemed, restored] spirit there is no [longer any] deceit!" (Ps. 32:1-2 NASB). Quoting these very words in his letter to the Romans, Paul wrote "Just as David...speaks of the blessing upon the man to whom God reckons righteousness apart from works," an imputed righteousness upon "the one who does not work, but believes in Him who justifies the ungodly, [whose] faith is reckoned as righteousness" (Rom. 4:6,5 NASB).

Consequently, David could sing: "Bless the LORD, O my soul; and all that is within me, bless His holy name. ... Who pardons *all* your iniquities...who redeems your life from the pit.... As far as the east is from the west, so far has He removed our transgressions from us" (Ps. 103:1,3-4,12 NASB). I am glad David did not write, "*As far as the north is from the south*, so far has He removed our transgressions from us," for the distance from the North

Pole to the South Pole can be measured, but the span separating the east from the west is a distance *without measure*! If I should begin walking, or flying, east today, I would *still be going east* ten trillion years from now, having circled the earth countless times over. I would be always going east, never reaching west. Hallelujah to the Lamb slain from the foundations of the world! He has removed our transgressions from us "as far as the east is from the west"!

Indeed, "the LORD sustains all who fall, and raises up all who are bowed down. ... My mouth will speak the praise of the LORD; and all flesh will bless His holy name forever and ever" (Ps. 145:14,21 NASB; David's final song of praise in our Book of Psalms).

I believe Ezra, in First Chronicles 20, recorded nothing of the details of David's sin because he, writing some 500 years after the actual events of David's double crimes of adultery and murder, clearly saw and solidly believed in the redemptive work in David's life. Ezra wrote in his chronicles just as if there had been no adultery staining David's soul and no bloodshed staining his hands. Praise God!

Taking a Step of Faith

I take these words as my step of faith this very day:
> *Lord Jesus, I long to be perfectly whole,*
> *I want Thee forever to live in my soul;*
> *Break down every idol, cast out every foe,*
> *Now wash me, and I shall be whiter than snow.*

Lord Jesus, let nothing unholy remain,
Apply Thine own Blood and remove every stain;
To get this blest washing I all things forego;
Now wash me, and I shall be whiter than snow.

Lord Jesus, Thou seest I patiently wait;
Come now, and within me a new heart create;
To those who have sought Thee Thou
  never saidst No!
Now wash me, and I shall be whiter than snow.

The blessing by faith I receive from above.
O glory, my soul is made perfect in love!
Your grace has prevailed, and this moment I know
The Blood is applied, I am whiter than snow.

— *James Nicholson*

Day Twenty-two

The Tragic Consequences of Unhealed Wounds

▶ Scripture Reading: 2 Samuel 13 through 19

*Now it was after **this** that Absalom the* [third eldest] *son of David had a beautiful sister whose name was Tamar, and Amnon the* [firstborn] *son of David loved her.*

2 Samuel 13:1

It is a painful fact that, notwithstanding the overwhelming forgiveness of God, we are not always able to see the human consequences of our sins reversed. Perhaps this is because sin is often the fruit borne by a whole inner root system of brokenness and pain, and this root system usually has long grown and pervaded and damaged many of the lives that surround us. I believe this was true in the life of David Ben Jesse. His adulterous sin with Bathsheba and his consequent murder of Uriah, her husband, were only the tip of a great iceberg of an as yet unhealed inner dysfunction.

The richest part of David's life was clearly his love for Jehovah. The one great psalm of David's life (Psalm 18; recorded initially in Second Samuel 22), begins with the passionate outburst, "*I love you*, O LORD, my strength" (Ps. 18:1). The most impoverished part of David's life, however, was his interpersonal human relationships. With the possible exception of Jonathan (and that relationship was cut short in death), David found it virtually impossible to love others in a productive, enduring way. Bathsheba may have felt herself flattered by David's attraction to her, but according to First Chronicles 3:1-9 and 14:3-7, six wives preceded her, and perhaps many more succeeded her as the objects of David's passion. The fact of the matter was that David did not know how to rightly love any woman or to give himself totally to her. That is why he multiplied wives and went from woman to woman.

In our previous chapters, we omitted the tragic happening of First Chronicles 15:29, the heartbreaking story of how "as the ark of the covenant of the LORD was entering the City of David, Michal daughter of Saul watched from a window. And when she saw King David dancing and celebrating, she despised him in her heart." Combined with this is the comment in Second Samuel 6:23, which adds this sad note to the story: "And Michal daughter of Saul had no children to the day of her death." Many contemporary observers have flippantly rushed in to judge and thereby misjudge Michal, but I believe an examination of the scriptural facts will prevent them from doing this any longer.

Michal was an emotionally battered woman. She had been used as a political pawn, first by her father Saul to destroy David (see First Samuel 18:20-25) and then more recently by David himself who, according to Second Samuel 3:12-16, took her from Paltiel, her brokenhearted second husband of some seven years, simply to make a favorable impression on the northern tribes of Israel who were still faithful to the house of Saul. This pagan practice of using women as political pawns became the snare that destroyed Solomon, David's eventual heir, with his many politically motivated marriages with women from the surrounding pagan kingdoms (see I Kings 3:1-3; 11:1-10). Solomon followed in his father David's footsteps to his own undoing.

On that day Michal despised David in her heart as she saw him leaping and dancing before the ark of Jehovah in the sight of a group of gaping slave girls because her own heart had been broken by David's cruel insensitivity to her. She resented his selfless love for Jehovah when he had none for her, and she resented the threat presented by those enthralled slave girls. This maxim is true: Hurting people hurt other people. I am personally, likewise, not quick to judge Michal's childlessness as *Jehovah's* judgment on her. She may have been childless because David feared Michal's rage, and rather than risk having contenders to his throne from the house of Saul, David refused to sleep with her from that day on. At best, Michal was an abused wife who deserves more of our compassion than our surface evaluations of her have at times allowed.

Young Amnon was David's firstborn and the heir to his empire. But the crown prince followed in the steps of his fallen father. The Hebrew text of Second Samuel 13:1 begins the fateful story of Amnon's fall with the statement, "*And* it happened afterward...." It clearly links the forthcoming events in Amnon's life to the prior fall in David's life, recorded in the previous chapter. Amnon lusted for his half-sister Tamar, and with the help of his cousin Jonadab he conceived of a way to seduce her. Disregarding her unflinching objections, Amnon, "since he was stronger than she...raped her" (2 Sam. 13:14). Then, as is often the case in situations like these, as he looked at her, sobbing and broken, "Amnon hated her with intense hatred. In fact, he hated her more than he had loved her" (2 Sam. 13:15). She would live the rest of her life in her brother Absalom's house, a desolate woman. Consequently Absalom came to hate Amnon his half brother because he had disgraced his sister Tamar. (Absalom apparently dearly loved his sister Tamar, enough for him to name his only daughter after her [2 Sam. 14:27]). We are further told that "when King David heard all this, he was furious" (2 Sam. 13:21), but apparently David fumed privately and could not bring himself to address this horrendous sin and its consequences. Perhaps he had not yet fully worked through his own shame over his grievous sin with Bathsheba. David apparently never did console Tamar in her devastation; he never did punish Amnon for his sin; and he never did calm Absalom in his rage. Consequently, two years later, in a carefully planned plot, Absalom had Amnon the crown prince assassinated. Then Absalom fled from Jerusalem to his grandfather Talmai, King of Geshur, a little Syrian principality in the Golan, where he remained in self-imposed exile for three years. Surprisingly, every day of those three years, we are told that David mourned for his son Absalom. Finally Joab, David's war-chief, seeing the deep grief of David, took measures to convince David to allow him to go to Geshur and bring Absalom back to Jerusalem. David's only request was that "'he must go to his own house; he must not see my face.' So Absalom went to his own house and *did not see the face of the king*" (2 Sam. 14:24). Absalom would be banished for yet another two years. Only after seven full years did David have a brief reconciliation meeting with Absalom, but by that time the dam inside of Absalom had broken and the bitter waters of his own rejection and of David's neglect were flooding his soul.

Someone once made the observation that some children would rather commit murder to get their parents' attention than to go on without it. Similar things were welling up within Absalom's heart. He planned and staged a successful *coup d'état* in which he forced his father David into exile, causing David to leave Jerusalem and his royal palace behind. During that time David suffered the loss of a number of his faithful subjects, including his close counselor Ahithophel. But it was Joab, David's war-chief, who finally brought this whole insanity to a halt. On one fateful day when fleeing on his mule from Joab and his men, Absalom got hung by his hair in the spreading branches of a large oak tree. Dangling between heaven and earth, Absalom was speared through the heart by Joab with three javelins and then hacked to death by ten of Joab's armor-bearers. They then "threw him into a big pit in the forest and piled up a large heap of rocks over him..." (2 Sam. 18:17). Their barbaric treatment of Absalom revealed their deep hatred for Absalom over his revolt.

In contrast, the grief of David over the death of Absalom is heartwrenching. Just listen to David's wailings: "O my son Absalom! My son, my son Absalom! If only I had died instead of you—O Absalom, my son, my son!. ... O my son, Absalom! O Absalom, my son, my son!" (2 Sam. 18:33; 19:4) In the depth of my heart of hearts I am compelled to ask David these questions: "Why did you never tell Absalom how much you loved him when he was alive? What was there in your own broken life that all but destroyed your ability to be a loving husband and a caring father? Why could you not translate into human expression toward your family something of the vast, divine, fatherly love you were beginning to find in Jehovah's presence? How could you be so eloquent in your love for Jehovah and yet so impoverished in the expression of your love for your sons?" Someday, in the eternal kingdom, I want to hear David's answers to my questions, for they are Absalom's questions, Amnon's questions, Tamar's questions, and Michal's questions too—and perhaps the questions of those who surround your life and mine!

Yes, there are consequences of sin; in particular, there are consequences of those hidden roots of dysfunction for which the acts of sin are but the fruit. Wounded people wound people, and they in turn wound other people. This is what happened with David, Amnon, Tamar, and Absalom. So the word of the Lord through the prophet Nathan was grievously fulfilled: "'Now, therefore, the

sword will never depart from your house...'" (2 Sam.
12:10). The prayer that David prayed in Psalm 51 at this
sad season in his life yet waits to be answered, but *it shall
be answered*: "Surely You desire *truth in the inner parts*....
Create in me *a pure heart*, O God, and renew a steadfast
spirit within me" (Ps. 51:6,10).

Yes, David, in the depths of his yet unhealed heart, had
touched the forgiveness of God: "You are forgiving and
good, O LORD, abounding in [covenant] love to all who call
to You" (Ps. 86:5). But now he awaited the fulfillment of
his deeper desire: ":..I will walk in Your truth; give me *an
undivided heart*, that I may fear Your name" (Ps. 86:11).
Asaph's epitaph over David's life shall also yet ring true:
"And David shepherded [Israel] with *integrity of heart*"
(literally, with a complete, entire, and perfect heart) (Ps.
78:72a). David's own repentant cry concerning his broken
family situation will also yet come to pass: "I will be
careful to lead a blameless life...I will walk in my house
with blameless heart [with integrity of heart]" (Ps. 101:2).

Taking a Step of Faith

*Father, You have forgiven me; now I want You to
transform me. Unite my divided heart, O Lord! Heal me
inwardly by Your sanctifying power and begin to heal my
relationships—my immediate family and the whole of my
family tree. Let the healing waters begin to flow into my
soul, and then out to others! By the grace of our Lord
Jesus Christ! Amen.*

Day Twenty-three

The Lust We Often Applaud

▶ Scripture Reading: 1 Chronicles 21

Satan rose up against Israel and incited David to take a census of Israel.

I Chronicles 21:1

There have been times, as I have paged through Christian magazines, that I have become queasy in the pit of my stomach as I noted men and women of God putting themselves forward by self-congratulating advertisements, by superlative claims and titles, and by descriptions of awesome spiritual feats in their ministry. Various ones have "the fastest growing church" in their area; others have brought "tens of thousands" to Christ. Some are influential "apostles" over an impressive number of churches; others are profound healers and sign-workers, and so on. We shrink in horror—and rightly so—when men and women of God succumb to sexual lust, but unfortunately, this self-glorification is also a lust—a lust for recognition—and one we often applaud in the Body of Christ. We are quick to congratulate the seemingly impressive successes of men and women of God, but I wonder how much of these self-advertisements are really not much more than an expression of broken personalities seeking to find their identity in their successes. I wonder how much of it is a cover-up, or a compensation, for a deep inner sense of personal failure in other areas of life. The honor we thus seek to generate by parading ourselves and our giftings is but pride dressed in another suit, a projection of unbroken self. Perhaps I am keen to detect this sickening practice because I myself have engaged in it. And I sense it may well be what motivated David to take a census of Israel.

A mystery hangs over not only *what* exactly motivated David to take that census, but also *who* exactly motivated him to do it. Over the objections of his war-chief Joab, David commanded, "Go and count the Israelites from Beersheba to Dan. Then report back to me so that I may know how many there are" (1 Chron. 21:2b). We are told that "the king's command was repulsive" to Joab (1 Chron. 21:6)—hence his response, "'Why does my lord want to do this? Why should he bring guilt on Israel?' The king's word, however, overruled Joab..." (1 Chron. 21:3-4).

The census took the greater part of a year. Joab's primary purpose was to count *the fighting men of Israel*, and the impressive tally came in at well over one million able-bodied men! This was surely a far cry from David's original 400 gathered in the cave of Adullam, his 600 at Keilah, and even the third of a million fighting men assembled some years before at his coronation. In all this we are compelled to ask whatever could David's motivation have been in such a seemingly rash act? He certainly had no fear of losing any of his battles, for the preceding three chapters record David's successes in one military campaign after another. Twice we are told that "the LORD gave David victory *everywhere* he went" (1 Chron. 18:6,13). I am, therefore, led to the conclusion that David found it necessary to know he had "the fastest growing" army in the Middle East because there were yet unmet insecurities in his soul, and this information would give a boost to his sense of personal identity. David was a man who could surely find a sense of security in his awesome attainments; they were many and mighty.

But the Lord has not constructed us to be fulfilled in that way. My identity, my personal self-worth, and my value ultimately cannot rest in what I do or even in what or who I am, but rather in *whose* I am! Hear David admonishing his choir director, perhaps on the backdrop of the painful lessons learned in that fateful census year:

> May *the LORD* answer you when you are in distress; may *the name of the God of Jacob* protect you. ... May *He* give you the desire of your heart and make all your plans succeed. We will shout for joy when you are victorious and will lift up our banners in the name of *our God*. May *the LORD* grant all your requests. *Now I know* that *the LORD* saves His anointed; *He* answers him from His holy heaven with the saving power of *His* right hand. Some trust in chariots and some in horses, but we trust *in the name of the LORD our God*. They are brought to their knees and fall, but we rise up and stand firm" (Psalm 20:1;4-8).

David's command to number Israel was indeed "evil in the sight of God; so He punished Israel" (1 Chron. 21:7). In the realization of what he had actually done, "David was conscience-stricken after he had counted the fighting men, and he said to the LORD, 'I have sinned greatly in what I have done...I have done a very foolish thing'" (2 Sam. 24:10).

As David watched 70 thousand of his men fall in Israel by the hand of the Lord's judgments (thus diminishing by nearly a tithe the numbers he had so gloried in), David emerged as a very repentant and subdued man. Hear what may well have been the cries of his heart:

> Out of the depths I cry to You, O LORD; O LORD, hear my voice. Let Your ears be attentive to my cry for mercy. If You, O LORD, kept a record of sins, O LORD, who could stand? But with You there is forgiveness; therefore You are feared. ... O Israel, put your hope in the LORD, for with the LORD is unfailing love and with Him is full redemption. He Himself will redeem Israel from all their sins (Psalm 130:1-4;7-8).

> My heart is not proud, O LORD, my eyes are not haughty; I do not concern myself with great matters or things too wonderful for me. But I have stilled and quieted my soul; like a weaned child with its mother, like a weaned child is my soul within me. O *Israel, put your hope in the LORD both now and forever more*" (Psalm 131).

All that we shall ever need of identity, of self-worth, of value, of acceptance, and of love is to be found in this one simple, timeless truth: "Jesus loves me this I know, for the Bible tells me so; little ones to Him belong; they are weak but He is strong." The key to inheriting this vast inner treasure is simply to become as that little "weaned child" of Psalm 131, for Jesus taught us that unless we become like little children we shall "never enter the kingdom of heaven" (Mt. 18:3).

The second issue of exactly *who* motivated David to number Israel also remains a mystery. First Chronicles 21:1 states "*Satan* rose up against Israel and incited David to take a census of Israel." But Second Samuel 24:1 (one of Ezra's historical sources) states, "Again the anger of the LORD burned against Israel, and *He* incited David against them, saying 'Go and take a census of Israel and Judah.'" Who, then, incited David—Jehovah or Satan? Our best conclusion is that the Lord used Satan, as He frequently does, to be His errand boy. So both accounts are accurate.

The statement in Second Samuel 24, "*Again* the anger of the LORD burned against Israel," glances back to the last historical event recorded in Second Samuel 21 before this present happening, to the time when "there was a famine for three successive years; so David sought the face of the LORD. The LORD said, 'It is on account of Saul and his blood-stained house; it is because he put the Gibeonites to death'" (2 Sam. 21:1). The issue in this other national judgment was that the Lord had not forgotten the treaty Joshua had made with the Gibeonites more than 400 years before (see Josh. 9), which Saul had broken, for "Saul in his zeal for Israel and Judah had tried to annihilate [the Gibeonites]" (2 Sam. 21:2c). To make amends, David had to turn over seven of Saul's sons and grandsons who were then killed "before the LORD" by the offended Gibeonites. Thus the famine was lifted. David, however, took great care in all of this to spare "Mephibosheth son of Jonathan, the son of Saul, *because of the oath before the LORD between David and Jonathan son of Saul*" (2 Sam. 21:7). In both of these acts—the sparing of Mephibosheth and the making of amends to the Gibeonites—David took great care to honor covenant, something Saul had failed to do and something for which Israel as a nation paid dearly.

I wondered, as I read over this account, how many of our own national calamities, with more yet to come, are directly connected to the Lord's anger over the 450 treaties that the United States government made and then broke with the original inhabitants of our land, the Native Americans. Add to that the bloody holocaust on our American soil of tens of millions of Native Americans slain, as well as millions of African American slaves killed, and now the holocaust of tens of millions of defenseless pre-born baby boys and girls aborted in death. For all this bloodshed, we are surely to be held dearly accountable by a holy and just God in Heaven. Perhaps in this light we can better interpret the floods, the droughts, the forest fires, the drugs, and the unprecedented violence in our land in which the innocent suffer along with the guilty. We in America are reaping what we have sown, just as Israel did. May we, as the Lord's royal priesthood, begin to come before Him to pray with humility and in repentance of soul so that *He might, through us, begin to heal our land* (2 Chron. 7:14)!

It was undoubtedly a similar national issue in Israel that caused the words to be written, "*Again* the anger of the LORD burned against Israel." The Lord, in judgment against Israel's national sins, apparently permitted Satan to incite David to number the people.

The sword of the Lord was a double-edged sword. His judgment was against Israel for her sins and against David for the pride of his heart. But David bitterly cried out to the Lord even as "God sent an angel to destroy Jerusalem. But as the angel was doing so, the LORD saw it and was grieved because of the calamity and said to the angel who was destroying the people, 'Enough! Withdraw your hand.' The angel of the LORD was then standing at the threshing floor of Araunah the Jebusite" (1 Chron. 21:15).

Taking a Step of Faith

*Lord Jesus Christ, I come to You this day for the healing of the ground within my own life. I am believing You for a redemption beyond forgiveness. I am believing You for a restoration in the broken places of my soul and in those broken places of my whole family. In the strength of what You are doing in me, I believe You will use me in a wider sphere—in the healing of our broken nation, our broken continent, our broken world. Make me an agent of Your reconciliation between Blacks and Whites, and Native Americans, Asians, and Hispanics and all other races! Gladly do I give of myself to this end, to see **You** pick up **Your** seamless "coat of many colors" and wear it for all the world to see! In Your dear name! Amen.*

Day Twenty-four

God of the Second Chance

► Scripture Reading: 1 Chronicles 22

> ..."The LORD, the LORD, the compassionate and gracious God, slow to anger, abounding in [covenant] love and faithfulness...and forgiving wickedness, rebellion and sin...."
>
> *Exodus 34: 6-7*

When David and the elders of Israel looked up and saw the angel of the Lord standing between heaven and earth with his sword drawn over Jerusalem in a stroke of judgment against David's arrogance in numbering his fighting men, they fell on their faces before Jehovah. With deep cries of repentance, David pled for the mercy of God to be extended to the innocent people of Jerusalem. And "the LORD, the LORD [was] compassionate...forgiving wickedness, rebellion and sin." The angel's sword stopped in midair; then the command was given through Gad, David's personal seer, to build an altar of sacrifice to the Lord on that very spot, which happened to be the threshing floor of Araunah the Jebusite.

The Jebusites had originally held the whole of Jerusalem as their impenetrable fortress, but David had defeated them some decades earlier and taken Jerusalem from them. Ornan [the post-exilic pronunciation of Araunah] was a Jebusite not expatriated in the conquest; he was permitted to remain and keep his farm and his threshing floor on this mount. This mount is identified for us in Second Chronicles 3:1 as "*Mount Moriah*, where the LORD had appeared to...David...on the threshing floor of Araunah the Jebusite...." This was indeed a wondrous place, an awesome place, a sacred place—the ancient dwelling of the great Melchizedek and the very site on which the patriarch Abraham had offered up his beloved son Isaac. David immediately purchased at full price the threshing floor from Araunah, who would have gladly given it to David for nothing. But David's response was, "I will not take for the LORD what is yours, or sacrifice a burnt offering that costs me nothing" (1 Chron. 21:24).

Second Samuel 24:24 records that David paid "fifty shekels of silver" (just over $100) for the threshing floor and the oxen that he then burnt as an offering before Jehovah. First Chronicles 21:25, however, records that "David paid Araunah six hundred shekels of *gold* [over $90,000] *for the site*." David, on the heels of his initial purchase of the threshing floor, had then bought the whole eight acres of Mount Moriah from Araunah! Something was obviously stirring in David's heart, something of the original passion that had stirred within his being some years before when Jehovah spoke to him about His building an everlasting house for David. David would now, at last, build a house for Jehovah on this very spot—at this very place of Heaven's merciful intervention! Had not the Lord intervened from Heaven and spared Isaac on this mount? Had not He now, likewise, intervened from Heaven and spared the sons and daughters of Isaac from the sword of destruction? Of course! What better place could there be for a house for Jehovah's excellent glory? Here in this very place Jehovah's mercy had triumphed over judgment (see Jas. 2:13)! Here God had become for David *the God of the second chance*! What better place could there be to celebrate a God whose "[covenant] love endures forever"? In the days to come, concerning God's people, Solomon would pray: "When they sin against You—for there is no one who does not sin—and You become angry with them...and if they have a change of heart...then from heaven, Your dwelling place, hear their prayer and their pleas.... And forgive Your people, who have sinned against You" (2 Chron. 6:36-37,39).

This indeed would be the place for the forgiveness of God to be received and celebrated always! Besides, who would dare go up to Gibeon to the tabernacle that Moses had made? Certainly not David, for he was afraid to go up to Gibeon because "of the sword of the angel of the LORD" (1 Chron. 21:30). But here at Zion David was safe, overshadowed by the tender mercies and compassions of Jehovah! Moses' tabernacle was framed and fashioned at the base of Mount Sinai, where 3,000 people fell by the sword on one day because of their sin (see Ex. 32:19-28). It's little wonder that David feared to go to the tabernacle, dreading "the sword of the angel of the LORD"! But Mount

Zion would be the place of redemption, the place where 3,000 people would be saved by the power of God on another, more glorious future day (see Acts 2:29-41). Indeed, it was only logical that "the house of the LORD God [was] *to be here*, and also the altar of burnt offering for Israel" (1 Chron. 22:1).

An interesting Jewish tradition describes what happened when Araunah originally "turned and saw the [destroying] angel; his four sons who were with him hid themselves" (1 Chron. 21:20). According to this Jewish tradition, they hid themselves in a cave under the rock over which the Holy of Holies was later constructed and which can still be seen under the Dome of the Rock on the Temple Mount in Jerusalem! This site was indeed a place of merciful refuge.

> So David gave orders to assemble the aliens living in Israel, and from among them he appointed stonecutters to prepare dressed stone for building the house of God. He provided a large amount of iron to make nails for the doors of the gateways and for the fittings, and more bronze than could be weighed. He also provided more cedar logs than could be counted, for the Sidonians and Tyrians had brought large numbers of them to David (1 Chronicles 22:2-4).

We have already commented on the tons of silver and gold that David provided from the spoils and from the tribute money, pouring them into the treasury of Jehovah for "the house to be built for the LORD should be of great magnificence and fame and splendor in the sight of all the nations" (1 Chron. 22:5b)! This would be David's finest hour. Mercy had triumphed over judgment. David would now be able to bring personal treasure out of those places of darkness in his life. The Lord would make *all* things—both the holy and the unholy—work together for David's good, for he was a man who loved God and had been called according to God's purpose (see Rom. 8:28).

As David, in his ecstasy, described the future temple to be one "of great magnificence and fame and splendor in the sight of all nations," he also mentioned his "son *Solomon*...young and inexperienced" (1 Chron. 22:5). It was he who would succeed David on the throne. Young Solomon would eventually construct the Lord's house and rule over the Lord's empire; above all else, Solomon would be the channel through whom the messianic promises would flow as the mighty river of God's eternal purpose. Herein lies the greatest demonstration of God's redeeming grace, of His ability to organize His greatest victories in our lives out of our deepest defeats, for this Solomon was the *son of David and Bathsheba*. Their first child, conceived in the sin of adultery, died at birth; "...the LORD struck the child that Uriah's wife had borne to David..." (2 Sam. 12:15). But after the deaths of Uriah and the child, a deeply repentant David took Bathsheba as his wife and "she gave birth to a son, and they named him Solomon. *The LORD loved him; and because the LORD loved him, He sent word through Nathan the prophet to name him Jedidiah"* [*loved by the LORD*] (2 Sam. 12:24-25).

I sense at this juncture that we must bow low in the presence of our utterly redemptive God; He who is severe against sin, and rightly so, is also merciful and compassionate toward those who have fallen. He is *the God of the second chance*. He is *the God of reversals*. He causes mercy to triumph over judgment by reversing His judgments in our lives so they might actually become His very blessing! O, such an amazing God! Such an amazing grace! Yes, "David was the father of Solomon, *whose mother had been Uriah's wife*," Matthew tells us in his genealogy of Jesus the Messiah, the son of David (Mt. 1:6). Our Messiah would be called "Jesus, [the Lord saves], because He will *save His people from their sins*" (Mt. 1:21b). He will save them from the guilt of their sins, from the power of their sins, and even from the divine consequences of their sins. This Jesus is our Savior—mine and yours!

We conclude our meditation today with one final, staggering thought from Scripture. The Lord not only forgave David, but He also redeemed his deepest defeats, causing them to become his greatest accomplishments—as seen both in his son Solomon and in the temple site at Jerusalem. But beyond even that, the Lord then chose David to become *His standard of excellence* for evaluating all the other kings of Israel and Judah! Just listen to these mind-boggling, inspired words as He spoke to Solomon: "As for you, if you walk before Me in integrity of heart and uprightness, *as David your father did...*" (1 Kings 9:4). Then hear the Lord's words to Jeroboam, first king of northern Israel: "...you have not been *like My servant*

David, who kept My commands and followed Me with all his heart, doing only what was right in My eyes" (1 Kings 14:8). The Lord's word concerning Abijah, King of Judah, was similar: "...his heart was not fully devoted to the LORD his God, *as the heart of David his forefather had been. ... For David had done what was right in the eyes of the LORD and had not failed to keep any of the LORD's commands all the days of his life—except in the case of Uriah the Hittite"* (1 Kings 15:3,5; see also 1 Kings 15:11 concerning King Asa, and 2 Kings 16:2 concerning King Ahaz).

It is obvious that after David was forgiven and restored by God Himself, he then became God's model king, the standard by which all other kings would be evaluated in Jehovah's eyes! In every sense of the word, David was a new covenant man (just born before his time)—one into whose life all the new covenant blessings, grace, mercy, and redemption of our Father had been poured out. And so David's story brings great hope to our own hearts!

In my pastoral work in our local church and in my interactions with the Lord's people as I travel in the ministry, I have become deeply burdened over how many Christians are shipwrecked on the shores of life's experiences. Wrong choices, sinful choices, and indiscriminate choices have left many saints devastated. The Church, because of its lack of revelation into the redemptive purposes of God, has often compounded that devastation. Many fallen believers have little hope. Many fallen ministers cannot ever seem to get up again. Divorced and remarried people must be content to be second-rate citizens in many segments of the Kingdom of God. In any number of places forgiveness is scarce, while restoration—if it ever happens—is a rare phenomenon. Perhaps I am telling your story just now. There was a time some years ago when these words were my own biographical sketch. But I was found by the God of David, the God of all grace, and He is here today to be your restorer as well!

Taking a Step of Faith

(A step of faith from Jeremiah 18:1-6 for you to take on behalf of yourself or for you to take, in faith, on behalf of someone in need of God's restoration.)

Father, I come humbly to You in Jesus' name. You see my shipwrecked and devastated life. Sin and failure have left me broken on the wheel of life, but I trust You this day to pick up the marred clay of my life and remake me into another, even better vessel as it pleases You. I cast myself on Your amazing grace, that You shall do in me and for me what You did in and for Your servant David. Thank You, Father. Thank You. Amen.

Day Twenty-five

An Army of Anointed Worshippers

▶ Scripture Reading: 1 Chronicles 23 through 25

Sing to the LORD a new song, His praise in the assembly of the saints. ...let the people of Zion be glad in their King. Let them praise His name with dancing and make music to Him with tambourine and harp. ... May the praise of God be in their mouths and a double-edged sword in their hands.
Psalm 149:1-3, 6

First Chronicles 23 opens up for us a fascinating section of inspired Scripture, and it begins with this statement: "When David was old and full of years, he made his son Solomon king over Israel." Though it is difficult for us to create a totally accurate time line for the life of David, we believe that David's midlife crisis with Bathsheba probably happened in his early fifties—sometime around 1035 B.C. David died in his early seventies, having reigned over Israel for 40 years—7 in Hebron and 33 in Jerusalem (1 Chron. 29:27)—having begun his reign in his thirtieth year at Hebron. The 20 years between his grave moral lapse and his death—from his early fifties to his early seventies—were definitely the years of David's greatest productivity. First Chronicles 23—25 are a high watermark in the record of that fruitfulness.

We have already noted that David was a *king* and a *priest*, a priest after the order of Melchizedek. The focus of our present consideration is on David the *prophet*. The preface to David's "last words" in Second Samuel 23 declares that he was "*the man anointed* by the God of Jacob, Israel's singer of songs" ("*Israel's beloved singer*," margin) (2 Sam. 23:1c). David then testified of himself, "The Spirit of the LORD *spoke through me*; His word was on my tongue" (2 Sam. 23:2). David was obviously prophetic in his giftings, as his messianic psalms clearly evidence.

In this same last will and testament David also testified, "*Is not my house right with God? Has He not made with me an everlasting covenant, arranged and secured in every part?*" (2 Sam. 23:5a). The most important happening in these final 20 years of David's life was his personal and family restoration. I must believe that much of what the locusts had eaten in David's earlier years was genuinely restored to him in his latter years. His deep and thorough repentance, as we see reflected in his final admonitions to his son Solomon, held the key to this restoration. Listen to David's words: "And you, my son Solomon, acknowledge the God of your father, and serve Him with wholehearted devotion [*a perfect heart*, KJV; *a whole heart*, NASB] and with a willing mind, for the LORD searches every heart and understands *every motive behind the thoughts*..." (1 Chron. 28:9). Reflected in David's prayer for Solomon is his own deep inner recovery shining through: "And give my son Solomon *the wholehearted devotion* [*the perfect heart*, KJV; NASB] to keep Your commands, requirements and decrees..." (1 Chron. 29:19).

David was a man who came to see that motives *were* important ("every motive behind the thoughts") and that a "perfect heart" *was* essential if one was to obey all the Lord's "commands; requirements and decrees." Also, from David's son Solomon's testimony in his Book of Proverbs, we can see yet more of David's deep repentance. Solomon writes, "When I was a boy in my father's house...he [David] taught me...'keep my commands and you will live. ...'" (Prov. 4:3-4); and "Why be captivated, my son, by an adulteress? Why embrace the bosom of another man's wife? ... He will die for lack of discipline, led astray by his own great folly" (Prov. 5:20,23).

Thus we are able to appreciate and respect much more deeply the great work that Jehovah did *through* David in his final 20 years, once we have established the great work that Jehovah first did *in* David and *in* his family. "Is not my house right with God?" This was probably one of the most important questions David could have raised in his last will and testament, for this is the most valuable legacy a person can leave behind. We must believe that the Lord will make that possible for *us* to do as well!

According to David's "last words," he was God's *anointed singer*. He was also *the prophet* from Mount Zion, according to Peter in Acts 2:29-31. David was an *anointed prophetic worshipper* before the Lord! The final decisions of his life, recorded in First Chronicles 23–25 indicate that this was very much the case. First Chronicles 23:27 records for us "the last instructions of David." These instructions were that "the Levites were counted from those *twenty years old* or more." According to verses 2-5 of this same chapter, David had already "gathered together all the leaders of Israel, as well as the priests and Levites. The Levites *thirty years old* or more were counted, and the total number of men was thirty-eight thousand. And David said, 'Of these...four thousand are to praise the LORD with the musical instruments I have provided for that purpose.'" According to this passage, David first took a census of all the Levites. (Because David's motivation in *this* census was his concern for Jehovah's house rather than the pride of his own heart, Jehovah was pleased.) The 38,000 Levites counted, "thirty years old or more," were then assigned to various fields of needed service. Twenty-four thousand were to supervise the work of the Lord's house, both in its initial construction (with over 153,000 workmen laboring seven years; 2 Chron. 2:17-18 and 1 Kings 6:37-38), and then in its ongoing maintenance. Six thousand were to be officials and judges (or arbitrators) over this vast band of workers. Four thousand were to be gatekeepers, *and 4,000 were to dedicate themselves wholly to the task of praising the Lord*! But as David evaluated the results of this census and the projected distribution, he was concerned. There were *not enough Levites*! Moses had originally set the starting age for the Levites at 30 years, according to Numbers 4:35. David's final act, however, was to lower the starting age to 20, thus creating a virtual army of new Levites that could serve! What would he have them do? Besides the practical tasks in the temple, "they were also to stand every morning *to thank and praise the LORD*. They were to do the same in the evening.... They were *to serve before the LORD* regularly in the proper number and in the way prescribed for them" (1 Chron. 23:30-31)! David thus created an army of anointed worshippers! For such a great King as Jehovah, there must be ceaseless adoration and praise—and there must be an abundance of it!

In conjunction with this happening, First Chronicles 25 stands as one of the most impressive chapters in the Bible. If ever any section of Scripture reveals for us the heart of David, this chapter does. He assembled his war-chiefs to plan one of the greatest military strategies in Israel's history: to "set apart some of the sons of Asaph, Heman and Jeduthun," not for manning the catapults and the battering rams but "for the ministry of prophesying, accompanied by harps, lyres and cymbals..." (1 Chron. 25:1). Their battles would be won not by might nor by power but by the Spirit of the Lord (see Zech. 4:6)! The authoritative prophetic word coming forth in praise and adoration before the Lord and ascending into the heavens would immobilize and bind principalities, powers, and spiritual forces of evil; thus protecting and preserving the Temple of God, the city of Jerusalem, and the people of God from the attacks of the armies of the nations, the earthly counterparts of those heavenly forces of darkness. Of the people of God it would be spoken, "May the praise

of God be in their mouths and a double-edged sword in
their hands ... to bind...kings with fetters, [and] nobles with
shackles of iron, to carry out the sentence written against
them. This is the glory of all His saints. Praise the LORD"
(Ps. 149:6,8-9). To this end, then, Asaph and his sons
"prophesied under the king's supervision" (1 Chron. 25:2).
Jeduthun and his sons "prophesied, using the harp in
thanking and praising the LORD" (25:3). Heman and his
fourteen sons *and three daughters* (there was no gender
discrimination in this prophetic ministry) were likewise
dedicated "for the music of the temple of the LORD, with
cymbals, lyres and harps, for the ministry at the house of
God" (25:6). All together, as their ranks swelled, there
were 288 who were "*trained and skilled* in music for the
LORD"; these were the anointed teachers over the thousands
of students whom David had conscripted—all the prophetic
young Levites from 20 years old and up (25:7-8)! What a
Bible school! What a glorious place of training! It was
Jehovah's own *conservatory of prophetic worship and
spiritual warfare*!

First Chronicles 25:9-31 then lists for us 24 rounds, or
courses, of duty to be distributed by lot to all these many
students and their teachers. Various commentators have
given their opinions as to what these 24 courses were
intended to cover. I sense they probably would quite
evenly cover a 24-hour day! I somehow believe David's
original plan was to have prophetic praise and worship
ascending before the Lord's throne *24 hours a day*—all day
and all night, every day and every night! Never should
there be a time when Jehovah was not worshipped and

adored! I believe Psalm 134, the final "song of ascents," was written to encourage *the night shift!* "Praise the LORD, all you servants of the LORD *who minister by night in the house of the LORD.* Lift up your hands in the sanctuary and *praise the LORD*" (Ps. 134:1-2).

David the prophetic worshipper was coming to the close of his life. I believe his inner thoughts could have been easily articulated in the words of author Victor Hugo when he passed his own eightieth year:

> I feel in myself the future life. I am like a forest which has been more than once cut down. The new shoots are livelier than ever. I am rising toward the sky. The sunshine is on my head. The earth gives me its generous sap, but heaven lights me with its unknown worlds.
>
> You say the soul is nothing but the result of the bodily powers. Why, then, is my soul more luminous when my bodily powers begin to fail? Winter is on my head, but eternal spring is in my heart. I breathe at this hour the fragrance of the lilacs, the violets, and the roses as at twenty years. The nearer I approach the end, the plainer I hear around me the immortal symphonies of the worlds which invite me. It is marvelous, yet simple."[12]

The Lord had restored David. His earlier words had actually been a prophecy over his own life: "He restores my soul. He guides me in the paths of righteousness for His name's sake. ... Surely goodness and [covenant] love will follow me all the days of my life, and I will dwell in the house of the LORD forever" (Ps. 23:3,6).

Taking a Step of Faith

*Lord Jesus Christ, Great Shepherd, what You did for David I believe You will do for me! I believe the years that are yet ahead of me shall be my finest and most productive! I believe You shall fully redeem **all** that pertains to me and **all those** who are part of my life! For Your name's sake! Amen.*

Day Twenty-six

A Brilliant Administrator

▶ Scripture Reading: 1 Chronicles 26 and 27

...King David put them in charge...for every matter pertaining to God and for the affairs of the king.
I Chronicles 26:32

Paul in First Corinthians 12:28 mentions "those with gifts of administration." Administration is among the giftings given by the Holy Spirit to believers. We need administration for the efficient management of our households, our businesses, and our ministries in the Body of Christ. Nothing runs smoothly without it. David clearly had the Old Testament equivalent of that New Testament gift of administration; David was a brilliant administrator.

It is around this insight that this book itself was conceived. About a year before I had been invited to share at the men's retreat of a group of brothers from Long Island, New York, to whom I've felt a real sense of closeness in the Lord. I was asked to share something that would help these men bridge the gap between the sacred

183

and the secular in their lives. How easy it is for men to be stirred with zeal at a retreat, only to lose some or all of that fire as they step back into their workaday world of business, mortgage payments, and college funds for the kids. What could I say that would help these brothers retain their spiritual zeal in the midst of their secular callings? How could the secular be transformed into the sacred as "whatever [we] do, whether in word or deed, [we] do it *all* in the name of the Lord Jesus, giving thanks to God the Father through Him" (Col. 3:17)?

Little did my pastor friend realize, when he asked me to consider this subject, that I myself was wrestling with the very same issues in my own life as a pastor. The increasing burdens and the ongoing concerns of a growing congregation had begun to drain the joy out of my life, and being in the midst of a multimillion-dollar building project had only added to my grief. Why did I have to manage so much of the mundane affairs of God's Kingdom? As soon as I delegated certain responsibilities to others, new responsibilities grew up like weeds to command my attention. I found myself growing cynical and even resentful over my 60- and 70-hour workweeks, and the endless stream of details that it seemed "only I could take care of."

I had found myself envying our Lord for His simple life style—Jesus with His 12 followers, leisurely walking down the dusty roads of Galilee, speaking about the carefree lilies of the field and the sparrows that were the constant object of their Father's love. Why could not my life be so simple?

I had to simplify my life style! But how? I needed to spend more time in His presence! But how?

Whatever *did* Martin Luther mean when he said, "I have so much to do today I simply must spend *more time in prayer*"? How was that possible?

How could I translate these yearnings of my heart into my own daily experience? How could I translate the wonder of His presence into the mundane doings of my daily grind? How could my secular things become sacred things?

As I drove up to the men's retreat at the Delaware Water Gap in Pennsylvania on that beautiful autumn day, I turned these thoughts over and over in my heart. I *myself* needed answers to the very questions that my brothers were asking. As I drove through New Jersey en route to the Gap, I knew I was to speak about David. But, surprisingly, the things that came out of my mouth that weekend about David were *new* to me; revelation just seemed to explode within my heart. I remember beginning my first sharing with this thought: "In case you thought that David was such a man of God because he sat around all day playing his harp and writing worship songs, that is not true. David was an awesome empire builder and a brilliant administrator, and it was in the very *midst* of his extremely busy life that he developed and grew as a man of God's presence. As a man after God's own heart, David brought that sense of God's presence into every detail of his extremely busy and pressured life."

I can truthfully say that I left that retreat changed. My life would never be the same. If no one else was ministered to that weekend, I was. In a new way, David had become a mentor to me—mentoring me on how to be a good administrator of the business at hand, bringing the very joy of God's presence into all that I was doing because I was doing it in His name, for His sake, and with His anointing!

The first half of First Chronicles 26 concerns itself with "the gatekeepers." That would be a rather mundane task, but David made it a joy. The sons of Korah were gatekeepers, as well as part of the Levitical choir (see 1 Chron 26:1). They were the redeemed and recovered sons of the *Korah* of Numbers 16, if you can believe it! The name *Asaph* in First Chronicles 26:1 is an abbreviation of Ebi*asaph*, who was indeed the son of the rebellious Kohathite, Korah, according to First Chronicles 6:22-23. (He is not to be confused, however, with David's contemporary Asaph, the famous chief musician.) Little wonder David chose *the sons of Korah* to serve in the temple courts. David believed in God's ability to redeem people beyond their birth, their genealogy, their ancestry, and their own family and personal failings. These sons of Korah were the ones who, in turn, magnified their ministry of being doorkeepers:

> Better is one day in Your courts than a thousand elsewhere; I would rather be a doorkeeper in the house of my God than dwell in the tents of the wicked. For the LORD God is a sun and shield; the LORD bestows favor and honor [on doorkeepers and gatekeepers!]; no good thing does He withhold from those whose walk is blameless (Psalm 84:10-11, a psalm of the sons of Korah).

We also note with interest the inclusion of Obed-Edom and his family as gatekeepers in First Chronicles 26:4-8. Obed-Edom's lack of genealogy seems to indicate that this was Obed-Edom the Gittite, the redeemed Philistine of I Chronicles 13:13-14. David, himself part foreigner, would naturally relish the inclusion of men such as Obed-Edom in the wider purposes of God, a foretaste of the future in which the Gentiles would be freely grafted into the new commonwealth of Israel (see Eph. 2:11-22).

In his administration, David made *no distinction between the sacred and the secular. Everything* was for the glory of God; *every* mundane task was for His name's sake. There was to be no difference between "every matter pertaining to God" and "the affairs of the king." All that was done in the kingdom was to be for Jehovah! "Four thousand [were] to be gatekeepers and four thousand [were] to praise the LORD with the musical instruments..." (1 Chron. 23:5), but both groups were to radiate His joy in their service, for   "As God's people pay proper attention to their status as a worshipping community, the distinction between the sacred and the secular disappears" (Martin J. Selman, *1 Chronicles: An Introduction and Commentary*).[13]

David, as a wise administrator, also chose leaders who "were very capable" (1 Chron. 26:6-9). Even in his final year, David was still out *looking for "capable men"* (26:31) to fill responsible positions in the kingdom! Also, David *did not "micromanage."* When he delegated responsibility to others, they were "in charge" (see 26:20, 22, 24, 26, 32). In the next chapter, First Chronicles 27:25-31, the expression "in charge" is also used more than a dozen times. David had learned how to release responsibility *fully* into the hands of capable people. The last half of First Chronicles 26 deals with those who were *"in charge* of the treasuries of the house of God and the treasuries for the dedicated things" (26:20); they were Israel's accounting department. Regarding the sphere of their responsibility, we also note with interest this statement: "Some of the plunder taken in battle they dedicated for the *repair* of the temple of the LORD" (26:27). Though the temple had not yet been built, David had a *maintenance plan* in place for its repair and upkeep! That was wise forethought! Good administrators like David *think ahead.*

The conclusion of this section (First Chronicles 27:32-34) reveals yet more of the administrative genius of David: he wisely *surrounded himself with the right mix of people.* In his cabinet was Jonathan, David's uncle. He was a prophetic voice, a counselor, "a man of insight;" he was also a scribe, David's secretary of state. Then there was Jehiel, who was responsible for taking "care of the king's sons," an important task, especially in the grooming of David's heir. Ahithophel was David's personal counselor, but he would betray David during Absalom's uprising—and would then take his own life. Ahithophel would be succeeded by two priests, Jehoiada and Abiathar, the lone survivor of Ahimelech of Nob (see 1 Sam. 22:9-23). The military advisor in David's cabinet was his war-chief, "Joab...commander of the royal army." One other cabinet member is mentioned: "Hushai the Arkite" from south Ephraim, whose sole function was that he was "the king's *friend.*" David, in the midst of the many demands of his administration, felt his need for a personal companion, a friend, a confidant, someone who could *minister to him, encourage him,* and *fill his emotional tank* so he could carry his vast workload without suffering the burnout that comes from unreplenished depletion. David was a wise man in the choosing of his cabinet.

The extent of David's administrative genius is further revealed in the brief sketch of the kingdom's infrastructure in First Chronicles 28:1:

> David summoned all the officials of Israel to assemble at Jerusalem: the officers over the tribes, the commanders of the divisions in the service of the king, the commander of thousands and commander of hundreds, and the officials in charge of all the property and livestock belonging to the king and his sons, together with the palace officials, the mighty men and all the brave warriors.

David, in his 40-year reign, had taken Israel from being 12 disconnected groups of nomads to becoming a well-integrated society, with a vast administrative infrastructure that knit every segment of that society—on both sides of the Jordan—together into one of the most influential and cohesive empires of his time. His delight in the midst of the humdrum of all his mundane administrative duties was simply this: "...Yours, O LORD, is the kingdom; You are exalted as head over all" (1 Chron. 29:11). The kingdom was Jehovah's, and all that was done was done to promote His headship, His lordship, His kingship, and His good pleasure! This, ultimately, is why the Lord has chosen to bless His people with administrative gifts such as David had. Every segment of our lives represents a piece of His Kingdom—our homes, our businesses, our churches. He is a God who is ever calling order out of the chaos in all these areas, that our lives may reflect the beauty of His peace.

In its apostolic beginnings, the early Church drew its inspired structures from the anointed simplicity of the tabernacle of David (see Acts 15:14-17). In its post-apostolic complexity—caused, among other things, by numerical growth in every place—the post-apostolic Church unfortunately drew its structures from the pagan Roman Empire. Church historians are able to trace the close parallels between the organization of the Roman state and that of the post-apostolic Church. The result of that sad move was the Dark Ages and the near total collapse of anointed apostolic simplicity. I wonder what would have happened had the post-apostolic fathers taken the theocracy of David as their model? The ongoing history of the Church would have been vastly different, I suspect. Oh, for godly wisdom in all that *we* set our hands to do in *this* generation in the Lord's Kingdom!

Taking a Step of Faith

Father, I want my ordered life to reflect the beauty of Your peace. I take from Your hands an anointing in wise administration, that my home, business, and ministry in Your church will be well-managed under Your Lordship; for Yours, O Lord, is the Kingdom, and You are exalted as head over all! Amen.

Day Twenty-seven

The Inspired Architect
of God's House

▸ Scripture Reading: 1 Chronicles 28

*Then David gave his son Solomon...the plans of all
that the Spirit had put in his mind....*
                                        1 Chronicles 28:11-12

Jehovah has always cherished having a place to live.
To Him there is "no place like home." The dwelling place
of God, from its simplest beginnings in Genesis to its grand
finale in Revelation, has actually become the framework on
which the whole of inspired Scripture hangs. The unfolding
of scriptural history and revelation runs parallel to the
unfolding of a house for God! We know that no earthly
home could ever actually contain Him, "since the heavens,
even the highest heavens, cannot contain Him" (2 Chron.
2:6), but Jehovah has always wanted a dwelling place
among His people. He has always desired a home here on
the earth in order that He might be given to hospitality, that

He might meet with His people and speak face-to-face with them (see Ex. 25:22).

The first mention of a house for God appears quite unexpectedly in Genesis in the days of the patriarchs. Four times in the story of Abraham mention is made of *Bethel*, which literally is "the house of God" (see Gen. 12:8; 13:3). This thought is greatly amplified in the experiences of Jacob at the site of that ancient city of Luz, which had been renamed Bethel. There, in a dream, Jacob saw the ladder of God bridging heaven and earth (which Jesus, in John 1:51, said was He Himself!). In his excitement over this messianic revelation Jacob declared, "How awesome is this place! This is none other than *the house of God*; this is the gate of heaven." And so "Jacob took the stone he had placed under his head and set it up as a pillar and poured oil on top of it." (See Genesis 28:17-18.) Jacob then made this profound statement to the Lord: "And this stone which I have set up as a pillar will be *God's house*; and of all that You give me I will give You a tenth" (Gen. 28:22).

Bethel was a simple house—made up of just one stone! But it was at least a beginning. It was, nonetheless, an anointed house, for Jacob had poured oil on its top. Here, even before the law mandated it, tithes would be gathered, for with God's house always comes the financial responsibility for funding the upkeep of that house, the service that goes on at that house, and the hospitality that is extended from that house to all of Jehovah's guests—especially the poor and the needy brought in from the highways and byways of life.

The house of God in the days of the patriarchs was only one stone because it reflected God's dwelling in the *individual* lives of those patriarchs. Abraham, Isaac, and Jacob were Jehovah's *individual* living stones.

In the days of Moses, however, the people of God had become a complex nation. Though they were a pilgrim people, they were an intricate society close to two million strong. It was only fitting, therefore, that God's next house should, first of all, be a *mobile home* in order for Him to accompany his pilgrim people. But it was also necessary that His house be a structure more complex than the patriarch's single stone. The intricate details of the construction of the tabernacle are given for us in Exodus 25—40. It was a complex structure, yet constructed together to be a whole—just like the people it mirrored. Among the construction materials of the tabernacle were one and a half tons of gold and five tons of silver—a value of over 30 million dollars, given as a freewill offering by the people of God from the spoils of Egypt, the past due wages for their years of bitter service in Egypt.

Even as the history of the patriarchs in Genesis clustered around Bethel, so the history of the nation of Israel clustered around the tabernacle, as recorded in Exodus through First Samuel. However, as the dealings of God in the earth turned a corner in and through the life of David in Second Samuel and First Chronicles, so the house of God turned the same corner. The tabernacle of David, the place of simple and anointed worship, was the third home where Jehovah was pleased to dwell. What was going on in David's tabernacle was but a reflection of the new thing God was doing in Israel through David: raising up simple, anointed, prophetic worship before the Lord.

The fourth place of God's dwelling was the Temple, prepared by David and then erected by Solomon. Even as the people of God had been brought to their place of highest glory by David in his final years, and by Solomon, David's son, in the beginning of his reign, so the Temple, as the singular, most awesome dwelling place of Jehovah, reflected this glorious upswing (see 1 Chron. 11—29).

The fifth place of God's dwelling was the restoration temple built by Zerubbabel and Joshua in the days of Ezra and Nehemiah, and Haggai and Zechariah after Judah's 70 years of Babylonian captivity ended and the people of God were released to return to their land. Unfortunately, this was the only house God did not inhabit. His glorious presence never filled this temple; there was no ark, no Holy of Holies, and no Shekinah glory. All of heaven and earth held its breath in expectation until the next dwelling should appear.

The next and ultimate dwelling place of God is the person of our Lord Jesus Christ, for "the Word became flesh and made His dwelling [literally, *tabernacled*] among us. We have seen His glory [the very Shekinah presence that had not come to Zerubbabel's temple], the glory of the One and Only, who came from the Father, full of grace and truth" (Jn. 1:14). Paul wrote concerning Jesus, "For God was pleased to have all His fullness *dwell* in Him" (Col. 1:19), "for *in Christ* all the fullness of the Deity lives in bodily form..." (Col. 2:9). In the person of Jesus, God fully lives, fully moves, and fully has His being! Jesus is God's ultimate home! His life, as the tabernacle of God, is the theme of the good news in our New Testament.

The seventh and final dwelling place of God is *the extended person* of our Lord Jesus Christ: "...the church, which is His body, *the fullness of Him* who fills everything in every way" (Eph. 1:22-23). As God's people, we, in union with Christ, rise "to become *a holy temple in the Lord.* ...built together to become *a dwelling in which God lives by His Spirit*" (Eph. 2:21-22); we are called to be a people "filled to the measure of *all the fullness of God*" (Eph. 3:19). The Church, as God's holy habitation, is the theme of the balance of the New Testament.

It is this house that John sees in its perfected and glorified form in his Revelation:

> I saw the Holy City, the new Jerusalem, coming down out of heaven from God, prepared as a bride ["the bride, the wife of the Lamb"] beautifully dressed for her husband. ... "Now the *dwelling of God* is with men, and *He will live with them.* They will be His people, and God Himself will be *with them* and be their God" (Revelation 21:2-3).

Thus the original intent of God is fulfilled. What began in Genesis with *one stone*, will be perfected and completed as a glorious *city* in the days of Jesus' return. The house of God will have grown from a single stone to a complex tent, to a temple, and finally to a dazzling city! Then God, at last, shall have a home in which He can best dwell, a home among His people, a home *within His people* if you will, and a place where all the nations of the earth can come and visit Him (see Rev. 21:24-26)!

In this whole plan, David played a vital role in designing the great house of God in his day! David spoke to the assembled leadership of Israel in First Chronicles 28:2: "...I had it in my heart to build a house as *a place of rest* for the ark of the covenant of the LORD, for the *footstool of our God....*" David's desire was to build a house where God could come and just take off His shoes, so to speak, and put up His feet and relax: "a place of rest"; a place for the "footstool of our God"! David apparently saw the finished work of Christ; he saw the Lamb slain from the foundation of the world, for David had prophesied about Him in his psalms. David also saw that God's redeeming "work has been *finished* since the creation of the world" (Heb. 4:3) and that Jehovah now invites His people to enter with Him into *His rest* (see Psalm 95, a psalm ascribed to David in Hebrews 4:7).

So it was that "David gave his son Solomon the plans.... He gave him the plans of all that the Spirit had put in his mind..." (1 Chron. 28:11-12). The intricate design of the Temple was one responsibility David did not delegate to anyone else. According to First Chronicles 28:14-18, the minutest details were planned by David himself, right down to the weight of each item—each gold fork and each silver dish. This is the only instance we can find where David *micromanaged* a project; but it was *his* project, and he would do it very well! "'All this', David said, 'I have in writing from the hand of the LORD upon me, and He gave me understanding in all the details of the plan'" (1 Chron. 28:19).   This is David, the inspired architect of God's house!

In all the details mentioned, David especially singled out the cherubim of glory that covered the ark.   These he upgraded.   He also referred to them in a unique way.   We are told that David gave Solomon "the plan for *the chariot*, that is, the cherubim of gold that spread their wings and shelter the ark of the covenant of the LORD" (1 Chron. 28:18).   In this unique designation, I believe, David set the backdrop for Ezekiel's opening vision of the throne of Jehovah being borne along by the cherubim on a *chariot* of glory!

Paul, in his sermon in the synagogue at Pisidian Antioch, summarizes David's life in these choice words: "...David had served God's purpose in his own generation" (Acts 13:36a).   What an epitaph!   What words for us to covet for our own lives!   Oh, that we might serve God's purpose in *this* generation!   Arthur Wallis in his classic work *In the Day of Thy Power* inscribed these words: "If you would make the greatest success of your life, try to discover what God is doing in your time, and fling yourself into the accomplishment of His purpose and will."[14] God's purpose in David's day was the building of a house for His excellent glory.   God's purpose in our day is the same: building a house for His excellent glory!   It's not a house of gold, silver, wood, and stone, but "a spiritual house" built out of the "living stones" of men and women who have been quarried out of this world and fashioned by the transforming power of the Holy Spirit to be building material for God's living temple (see 1 Pet. 2:5). What a glorious purpose for us to give ourselves to in this prophetic end-time generation!

Taking a Step of Faith

Glorious Lord, I consecrate my life to You, to serve Your purpose, without compromise, in this generation! Use me to gather living stones and to shape them and build them into Your house, that You might have a magnificent place to dwell, a place to fill with Your excellent glory! In Jesus' name. Amen!

Day Twenty-eight

A Final Look Into David's Lavish Heart

▶ Scripture Reading: 1 Chronicles 29

In my devotion to the temple of my God I now give my personal treasures...over and above everything I have provided for this holy temple.

1 Chronicles 29:3

With pain I have watched various relatives begin the wrap-up of their sunset years. People who all their lives had otherwise been outwardly generous and giving, gradually began to take on an almost obsessive attitude toward their possessions. The insecurities of old age made them vulnerable to clutching their things, their money, and their investments. Suspicion always seemed to hang heavy in the air as to who was stealing from them, who was misappropriating their funds, who was diminishing their resources. Can it be that old age becomes the final revelation of what *really* lies deep within our hearts and souls? I suspect that if we actually *are* materialistic and self-centered at our core, old age will cause those negative qualities to manifest themselves without inhibition.

In David's life the opposite was true. His final acts were his most generous. The real David shone forth in his sunset years in some of the greatest expressions of what it meant to be a man after God's own lavish heart! Just listen to David's words:

> With all my resources I have provided for the temple of my God—gold for the gold work [3,750 tons of it], silver for the silver [37,500 tons of it], bronze for the bronze, iron for the iron [in such abundance it could not be weighed] and wood for the wood, as well as onyx for the settings, turquoise, stones of various colors, and all kinds of fine stone and marble—all of these in large quantities" (1 Chronicles 29:2).

We have already noted that David had accumulated from his military campaigns *over fifty billion dollars* worth of these materials for the Lord's house! Now, in the sunset years of his life, David could surely step back with a deep sense of accomplishment and retire from the scene. He had made some wise personal investments throughout his life, and now he was well-prepared for his retirement.

But wait! Just listen to David's further amazing statements:

> Besides, in my devotion to the temple of my God *I now give my personal treasures* of gold and silver for the temple of my God, *over and above*

everything I have provided for this holy temple: three thousand talents of gold (gold of Ophir) and seven thousand talents of refined silver, for the overlaying of the walls of the buildings, for the gold work and the silver work, and for all the work to be done by the craftsmen... (1 Chronicles 29:3-5).

Out of his own personal retirement funds, David gave 3,000 talents of gold—*the gold of Ophir*. The gold of Ophir was the finest in the world, and David gave out of his personal treasures 110 tons of it for the building of the Temple! Plus 7,000 talents of *refined* silver. Refined silver was *the finest* of its kind, and David personally gave 260 tons of it for the Lord's house! We are talking here of a $1.5 billion gift! I sense this is part of what it means that David was a man after God's own heart. Jehovah's heart is lavish and giving, and David's heart was like his Father's! David was a lavish giver in the cause of God.

I look back with joy at the time when we were taking "Project Glory" pledges for our new worship center, "a house for God's excellent glory." One evening as I was driving home with my nearly 90-year-old mother, we began to talk about the new building and about the pledges that were being taken for it. After a brief silence, my mother informed me that I was to take a certain sum of money out of her meager checking account and give it to "Project Glory." Initially, I wanted to talk her out of it, or at least persuade her that she could give it on a monthly basis out of her $585-a-month income; but mother wanted to give a lump sum because she wasn't sure how long she had to live, and she wanted to make sure it would all be given! I thought of our Lord's joy over the poor widow and her two mites. She too, like David, was a *lavish* giver! The Lord loves these kinds of *hilarious* givers! (See Second Corinthians 9:7, literal Greek).

David's generous giving started an avalanche of generous giving among the leadership of Israel. "Then the leaders of families, the officers of the tribes of Israel, the commanders of thousands and commanders of hundreds, and the officials in charge of the king's work *gave willingly*" (1 Chron. 29:6). They collectively gave 190 tons of gold, 375 tons of silver, 675 tons of bronze, and 3,750 tons of iron; in addition, "any who had precious stones gave them to the treasury of the temple of the LORD in the custody of Jehiel the Gershonite" (1 Chron. 29:8). Nearly $2.5 billion in gifts came in that day for the Lord's house!

The avalanche continued: "The people rejoiced...for *they* had given freely and wholeheartedly to the LORD. David the king also rejoiced greatly" (1 Chron. 29:9). Translator Kenneth Taylor in the Living Bible captures the joy of that moment with these words: "*Everyone* was excited and happy for this opportunity of service, and King David was moved with deep joy"! I believe this was one of David's finest hours—and one of Israel's finest hours!

In his inspiring prayer of dedication, we pick up something of the grand vision that filled David's heart at that time.

> Yours, O LORD, is the greatness and the power
> and the glory and the majesty and the splendor, for
> *everything in heaven and earth is Yours.* Yours,
> O LORD, is the kingdom; You are exalted as head
> over all. Wealth and honor come from You....
> Everything comes from You, and *we have given
> You only what comes from Your hand.* ... O LORD
> our God, as for all this abundance that we have
> provided for building You a temple for Your Holy
> Name, it comes *from Your hand*, and *all of it
> belongs to You.* I know, my God, that you test the
> heart and are pleased with integrity. All these
> things have I given willingly and with honest
> intent. And now I have seen with joy how
> willingly Your people who are here have given to
> You. O LORD, God of our fathers Abraham, Isaac
> and Israel, *keep this desire in the hearts of Your
> people forever, and keep their hearts loyal to You*
> (1 Chronicles 29:11-11,14,16-18).

What a awesome prayer! "...Everything in heaven and
earth is yours...[therefore] we have given You only what
comes from Your hand...[for] all of it belongs to You,"
David prayed. Communism is a miserably failed ideology
in the earth. Communism's basic tenet is that *everything
belongs to the state*, but that is wrong. It does not.
Capitalism is presently faring a bit better in the earth, but
it too, is imploding, collapsing in upon itself. It too shall
utterly fail, for its basic philosophy, that *everything belongs
to the individual*, is also wrong. It does not. Only the
Lord's Kingdom shall endure forever, for the basic tenet of
the Kingdom of God is that "everything in heaven and earth

is *Yours* [O LORD]...all of it belongs to *You*"! We are but stewards of what our Lord has given us. All that we have belongs to Him, and when we give *anything* to Him, "we have given...only what comes from [His] hand"; for "it comes from Your hand, and all of it belongs to You"!

Dotty and I can remember our very first holy convocation camp meeting in northern Minnesota. For several days of seeking God, people from various places had come to our simple campgrounds (the back field of our future home!). This was just months before our wedding, and Dotty had our future home, where she lived, already stocked with engagement presents. However, as people needed sheets, blankets, pillowcases, towels, knives, forks, and spoons...one by one the new packages were broken open and the precious supplies distributed. As Dotty was pensively standing in the kitchen, watching our brand-new possessions being distributed to those in need, an older sister in the Lord came over to her and gently said, "The sooner you realize that *none of it is really yours*, the happier you will be." I think that on that day, the tone for our whole future life together was set. It is all His. Everything is His. We are His. Our lives are His. Our home is His. Our children are His. Our finances are His. All our belongings are His. We are merely called to be good stewards of *His* possessions and to give back to *Him* whatever *He* needs, as *He* needs it, and whenever *He* needs it. When once you see this one solitary truth, consecration, service, and giving no longer become a struggle; they become a joy. "Everyone was excited and happy for this opportunity of service, and King David was moved with deep joy"!

Taking a Step of Faith

*Father in heaven, forgive me for thinking that anything I am or anything I have is my own. I declare this day in Your presence that all I have and all I am and all I ever hope to be is **Yours and Yours alone!** With no further hesitation I commit everything I am and all I possess to You to use as You please, for I am only a steward over my life, my abilities, and my possessions—Your steward! Take whatever You will, as You will, whenever You will. With joy I dedicate it **all** to You! In the holy name of Jesus my Lord! Amen.*

Day Twenty-nine

The Setting of the Sun

▸ Scripture Reading: 1 Kings 1 and 2
1 Chronicles 29:21-29

David the son of Jesse...died..full of...honor...
1 Chronicles 29:26-28 NASB

The lion king had aged; he was an old lion now. He had nearly lost his life in an earlier skirmish against the Philistines: "...David went down with his men to fight against the Philistines, and he became exhausted. ... But Abishai son of Zeruiah came to David's rescue... Then David's men swore to him, saying, 'Never again will you go out with us to battle, so that the lamp of Israel will not be extinguished'" (2 Sam. 21:15,17). I sense that David, in his zeal for Jehovah of hosts and in his zeal for life itself, was finding it hard to let go. But the strain of age was taking its toll. I personally have a hunch that David would have gone right on to build the temple of God itself had he not simply run out of days in his life. If I know David, he would have surely found a legitimate way to reverse the Lord's word:

"You are not to build a house for My Name, because you are a warrior and have shed blood" (1 Chron. 28:3)!

There are different times and seasons in life, each with its own glory. There is "a time to be born and a time to die," David's son Solomon wrote (Eccles. 3:2a). There is also a time to build and to do battle, and there is a time to turn things over for others to do the building and the battling. There is a glory in being young; there is also a glory in growing old. Perhaps David was finding it hard to let go of being a young builder and a youthful warrior, but he would now have to come to embrace the glory of his senior years.

The psalmist, probably David, wrote these words: "You have exalted my horn like that of a wild ox; fine oils have been poured upon me. My eyes have seen the defeat of my adversaries; my ears have heard the rout of my wicked foes" (Ps. 92:10-11). Then we note this shift in his words: "The righteous will flourish like a palm tree, they will grow like a cedar of Lebanon; planted in the house of the LORD, they will flourish in the courts of our God. *They will still bear fruit in old age, they will stay fresh and green, proclaiming, 'The LORD is upright*; He is my Rock, and there is no wickedness in Him'" (Ps. 92:12-15).

The young warriors who surrounded David feared that he would be cut down in battle and that "the lamp of Israel [would] be extinguished." They saw his higher value as a senior saint in his being a radiant, guiding lamp of testimony for all Israel to follow, especially for the young men. In Psalm 71, thought by commentators to be David's own words, the psalmist testified about his youth: "For You have been my hope, O Sovereign LORD, my confidence since my youth" (verse 5). But then the psalmist declared, "Even when I am old and gray, do not forsake me, O God, till *I declare Your power to the next generation, Your might to all who are to come*" (verse 18). David was now entering a season in which his glory would be in passing the flaming torch of testimony on to the next generation.

David's inability to let go at the proper time was probably what spurred Adonijah to seize the throne of Israel in the days just before David's death.

Who would be the declining David's heir? Why not Adonijah?

Adonijah was David's fourth son, probably his eldest living son, when he "put himself forward and said, 'I will be king'" (1 Kings 1:5). At age 35, Adonijah was a self-willed and unbroken man. He is a reflection of David's failure as a father. The inspired writer inserts into his record in First Kings 1:6 this parenthetical thought concerning Adonijah: ("His father had *never interfered with him* by asking, 'Why do you behave as you do?' He was also very handsome and was born next after Absalom.") In seeking support in this risky venture of seizing the throne, Adonijah, surrounded by members of the royal court, "conferred with Joab son of Zeruiah [David's war-chief] and with Abiathar the priest, and they gave him their support" (1 Kings 1:7). For their respective parts in seeking to usurp David's throne, all three would pay dearly.

Joab and Adonijah would be killed, and Abiathar would be set aside and replaced by Zadok as priest in the immediate days that Solomon, David's rightful heir, consolidated his throne (see 1 Kings 2:25,34-35).

Yes, Solomon had been chosen by Jehovah, and he would sit on the throne of David. For this reason, David charged Zadok the priest, Nathan the prophet, and Benaiah the son of Jehoiada to:

> ...set Solomon my son on my own mule and take him down to Gihon [the spring on the eastern slope of Mount Zion]. There have Zadok the priest and Nathan the prophet anoint him king over Israel. Blow the trumpet and shout, "Long live King Solomon!" Then you are to go up with him, and he is to come and sit on my throne and reign in my place. I have appointed him ruler over Israel and Judah (1 Kings 1:32-35).

So they "put Solomon on King David's mule and escorted him to Gihon. Zadok the priest took the horn of oil from the sacred tent and anointed Solomon. Then they sounded the trumpet and all the people shouted, 'Long live King Solomon!'" (1 Kings 1:38-39)

The first believers in Acts 4:25 ascribed the authorship of our second psalm to David. I cannot help thinking that David may have composed this messianic psalm around these very events of Adonijah's uprising. In Psalm 2 David reflects:

> Why do the nations conspire and the peoples plot
> in vain? The kings of the earth take their stand
> and the rulers gather together against the Lord

and against His Anointed One. ... The One enthroned in heaven laughs; the Lord scoffs at them. Then He rebukes them in His anger and terrifies them in His wrath, saying, "I have installed my King on Zion, My holy hill." [Then the rightful heir speaks:] I will proclaim the decree of the LORD: He said to me, "You are My Son; today I have become Your Father [see this of Solomon in First Chronicles 28:6-7]. Ask of Me, and I will make the nations Your inheritance, the ends of the earth Your possession. You will rule them with an iron scepter; You will dash them to pieces like pottery." ... [Then Jehovah admonishes the offenders:] Kiss the Son, lest He be angry and you be destroyed in your way, for His wrath can flare up in a moment..." [see this of Solomon in comparing First Kings 1:53 with First Kings 2:23-25] (Psalm 2:1-2, 4-9,12).

I am sure David, prophetic soul that he was, could see in Adonijah's usurping the throne and in the nation's temporary rejection of its rightful king the rejection of the greater Son of David. As David, from his window, watched Solomon being carried along on his own mule into the city of David to sit upon the throne of David, and as David thought of his son Solomon being anointed with holy oil and declared king amidst trumpet blasts and shouts of joy, I sense David's prophetic eye caught the still future event in which his greater Son would ride into the city of Jerusalem amid shouts of joy: "Hosanna to the Son of David! Blessed is He who comes in the name of the Lord!

Hosanna in the highest!" (Mt. 21:9b) Perhaps David also glimpsed how the prophetic word would come to pass: "Say to the Daughter of Zion, 'See, your king comes to you, gentle and riding on a donkey, on a colt, the foal of a donkey'" (Mt. 21:5)!

In First Chronicles 29:22-25 we are also told that for Solomon there was *a second coming* to the throne as they "acknowledged Solomon son of David as king *a second time*, anointing him before the LORD to be ruler and Zadok to be priest. So Solomon sat on the throne of the LORD as king in place of his father David. He prospered and...*all* of King David's sons, pledged their submission to King Solomon. [Note carefully these words:] The LORD *highly exalted Solomon* in the sight of *all* Israel *and bestowed on him royal splendor such as no king over Israel ever had before*."

How extremely prophetic! Jesus, the rejected future heir, rides into Jerusalem the first time on a donkey amidst shouts of acclaim as the blessed Son of David. Then in His second coming to the Holy City He is again hailed as king and permanently enthroned on the seat of David. Paul, in words nearly identical to Ezra's, also tells us, "*Therefore also God highly exalted Him, and bestowed on Him the name which is above every name*, that at the name of Jesus *every* knee should bow...and that *every* tongue should confess that Jesus Christ is Lord, to the glory of God the Father" (Phil. 2:9-11 NASB). Amen!

On Solomon's glad coronation day, Zadok, the "Righteous One," was also anointed before the Lord to be priest in the place of Abiathar the defector. For Zadok's loyalty to the throne of David, the house of Zadok will also appear a second time in the prophetic scheme of things as honored priests in the end-time Temple of Jehovah! (See Ezekiel 40:46; 43:19; 44:15; 48:11.) In that day the "descendants of Zadok...who faithfully carried out the duties of My sanctuary when the Israelites went astray from Me, are to come near to minister before Me; they are to stand before Me...declares the Sovereign LORD. They *alone* are to enter My sanctuary; they *alone* are to come near My table to minister before Me and perform My service" (Ezek. 44:15-16). This is an encouragement for *us* who loyally stand with *our* King, awaiting His second coming!

David has now finished his life's work. The sun is setting. The lamp of Israel is about to be extinguished. Ezra concludes the journey of David with this fitting epitaph: "David son of Jesse was king over all Israel. ... He died at a good old age, having enjoyed long life, wealth and honor..." (1 Chron. 29:26,28). The Hebrew words are even more powerful: "He died...*full of...honor*" (that is, "satiated, overloaded with honor"). The word *honor* used here is translated 170 times elsewhere in the Old Testament as "glory." David died *overloaded with glory—full, satiated with glory*! The Lord had redeemed His servant. Jehovah had restored David in *every* sense of the word.

It is true that the original vessel Jehovah had been shaping on His wheel was marred [literally, "ruined"] in His hands, but Jehovah had "formed it into another pot, shaping it as seemed *best* to Him" (Jer. 18:4). I can believe the second shaping was better than the first. It was God's "best."   God's seconds are always better than His firsts anyway. The second Man was more glorious than the first (see 1 Cor. 15:47); the second creation is more far-reaching than the first; the second birth is eternally better than the first; the second covenant is more powerful than the first; and so on many times over. What the Lord did for David, He can do for you and for me.   That is the foremost encouragement we can take from our journey with David, for our own journey from brokenness to wholeness. By faith, we are told in Hebrews 11:34, David was one of those "whose weakness was turned to strength." The Lord yearns to do that for us as well!

David died "full of days, riches and honor" (1 Chron. 29:28 NASB) and he was "buried in the City of David" (1 Kings 2:10). The sun had set—only to rise on the other side in a greater morning glory! But even in its setting, this sun long illuminated the darkening sky. As quoted in *Streams in the Desert*, Beecher says: "When the sun goes below the horizon, the heavens glow for a full hour after its departure. And when a great and good man sets, the sky of this world is luminous long after he is out of sight.   Such a man cannot die out of this world.   When he goes he leaves behind him much of himself. Being dead, he speaks."[15]

Taking a Step of Faith

*My Father, I am fully prepared to believe You for my life—that I shall serve Your purpose in this generation and that I shall be carried into Your presence **full of honor**! In*

*the balance of the days that You have assigned to my life,
I believe You will anoint me and enable me, as You did
David, to fulfill every one of the tasks You have appointed
for me to do. Give me the grace, when the time comes, to
know how to "let go" and to pass the mantle on to others.
For Jesus' sake. Amen.*

Day Thirty

The Truth That Sets Us Free

*You will know **the truth**, and **the truth** will set you free."*

Our Lord Jesus, John 8:32

We have completed our journey with David. As we have walked with him on his path from brokenness to wholeness, perhaps we have seen ourselves in some small measure in him, both in our need and in our recovery. One final word remains to be spoken—a word concerning the truth that set David free and that will set us free.

In every one of our lives, as in David's life, there are things that are *true*; some of these things are *devastatingly true*. These kinds of things can never set us free. As a matter of fact, the knowledge of them can cripple us, bind us, and enslave us. So it is not knowing, rehearsing, and confessing the things about ourselves that are *true* that set us free; it is the *truth* that sets us free. And the *truth*, simply stated, is what God says about us. That is *the truth* that sets us free! As a matter of fact, that truth will set us free from even those things about ourselves that are true!

So for our own eternal good, we must be people who *know the truth*, *confess the truth*, and *rehearse the truth* about ourselves—those things that our God Himself says are *the truth* about us!

Although it is *true* that David was a very dysfunctional man, *the truth* about David was that he was "like the man from on High." That is how the Lord saw him and that is what He called him. Although it is *true* that David was an adulterer and a murderer, *the truth* about David was that he was a blessed man because, in his repentance, his transgressions were forgiven and his sins were covered, and the Lord did not count his sin against him (see Ps. 32:2). That was the Lord's verdict on David's life, and that was *the truth*. Although it was *true* that David initially built weakness into his own family, *the truth* about David was that "from everlasting to everlasting the LORD's [covenant] love is with those who fear Him, and His righteousness with their children's children—with those who keep His covenant and remember to obey His precepts" (Ps. 103:17-18). This is what the Lord declared over David, and that was *the truth* that worked in David's family in order that David could say at the end of his days, "Is not my house right with God?" Indeed, "You will know *the truth*, and *the truth* will set you free"!

Commentators have long puzzled over the disparity between the sad account of David's life in Second Samuel and the glorious account of these same years of his life as recorded in First Chronicles. I myself initially almost could have thought that the Scriptures were describing two different Davids—the one of Second Samuel and the other of First Chronicles! The resolution, however, has now become simple: Second Samuel records what is *true* about David; First Chronicles is an account of *the truth* about David!

Along these lines, Isaiah gives a very interesting word to us concerning David in Isaiah 55. "Give ear and come to Me; hear Me, that your soul may live. I will make an everlasting covenant with you, My faithful [covenant] love promised to David. See, I have made him *a witness to the peoples*..." (Is. 55:3-4). David's witness, or testimony, is preserved for us, I believe, in the next statements in this precious fifty-fifth chapter. This, I believe, is David's own testimony from his own penitential experience: "Seek the LORD while He may be found; call on Him while He is near. Let the wicked forsake his way [as David did] and the evil man his thoughts [as David did]. Let him turn to the LORD [as David did], and He *will* have mercy on him, and to our God, for He *will* freely pardon" (Is. 55:6-7).

I am sure there are many voices who will legitimately rise up at this very juncture and ask why there was no probation period, no time of waiting to see if David really *meant* his repentance before he was redeemed and restored to God's presence and recovered to his place as king. I am sure *some* would even strongly question why David, as an adulterer and a murderer, should *ever* have been restored to the purposes of God! I sense that it is God Himself answering these concerns for us in the very next statements: "'For My thoughts are not your thoughts, neither are your ways My ways,' declares the LORD. 'As the heavens are higher than the earth [a limitless space in our expanding universe], so are My ways higher than your ways and My thoughts than your thoughts'" (Is. 55:8-9). This word of redemption is *the truth* that goes forth from the mouth of the Lord into the ears of every fallen soul of man and woman; this good news will not return to Him empty but will accomplish what He has sent it forth to accomplish (see Is. 55:11). All this "will be for the LORD's renown," Isaiah concludes (55:13). Paul put it this way: it will be for the "praise of His glorious grace, which He has freely given us in the One He loves. [For] in Him we have redemption through His blood, the forgiveness of sins, in accordance with the riches of God's grace that He lavished on us..." (Eph. 1:6-8).

It was David who coined that great phrase "the LORD...is good; His [covenant] love endures forever." These were David's grand themes of truth concerning Jehovah. They were to be declared both before the ark of His presence in Jerusalem and before the tabernacle of the Lord at the high place in Gibeon (see 1 Chron. 16:37-41). These anointed words would also be *the truth* that would bring the glory of God down from heaven at the dedication of the temple:

> ...Accompanied by trumpets, cymbals and other instruments, they raised their voices in praise to the LORD and sang: "He is good; His [covenant] love endures forever." Then the temple of the LORD was filled with a cloud, and the priests

could not perform their service because of the cloud, for the glory of the Lord filled the temple of God (2 Chronicles 5:13-14).

The message is simple but powerful: *The Lord is good!* How often the enemy has lied to us to get us to believe otherwise. How often, in the midst of the many disappointing and painful experiences of life, even when we have miserably failed God, Satan has then lied to us about our God, slandering Him in our ears. But the fact remains, the grandest truth of Holy Scripture is simply this: *Our God is good!* He is good to us! And His covenant love (*hesed*, Hebrew) endures forever! This Hebrew word *hesed* is used about 250 times in the Old Testament, and it means "loyal, steadfast, faithful, covenant love." Therefore, Jehovah can *always* be depended upon. He does not *ever* leave us or forsake us. His word of promise to us can *never* be broken. He is a God of faithful and unfailing covenant love! Twenty-six times in Psalm 136, "the Great Hallel," the grand confession is made that "His [covenant] love endures forever"! When we are tempted to speak negatively about our circumstances or about the God of our circumstances, let us exchange those ashes for the beauty of this confession: "His [covenant] love endures forever"! This is the most absolute truth in all Scripture! Our God is good and His covenant love endures forever!

In the midst of grave opposition and hurtful accusation, David speaks this truth: "But let all who take refuge in You be glad; let them ever sing for joy. Spread Your protection over them, that those who love Your name may rejoice in You. For surely, O LORD, You bless the righteous; You surround them with Your favor as with a shield" (Ps. 5:11-12).

Written to the tune of "The Death of the Son" (perhaps Absolom), David, apparently in the midst of one of the great losses in his life, testified to the truth: "The LORD is a refuge for the oppressed, a stronghold in times of trouble. Those who know Your name will trust in You, for You, LORD, have *never* forsaken those who seek You" (Ps. 9:9-10).

When David recounted his deliverance "from the hand of all his enemies and from the hand of Saul," these were his words: "It is God who arms me with strength and makes my way perfect. He makes my feet like the feet of a deer; He enables me to stand on the heights. He trains my hands for battle.... You give me Your shield of victory, and Your right hand sustains me; You stoop down to make me great" (Ps. 18:32-35).

Psalm 21 contains one of David's grandest testimonies:

O LORD, the king rejoices in Your strength. How great is his joy in the victories You give! You have granted him the desire of his heart and have not withheld the request of his lips. You welcomed him with rich blessings and placed a crown of pure gold on his head. He asked You for life, and You gave it to him—length of days, for ever and ever. Through the victories You gave, his glory is great; You have bestowed on him splendor and majesty. Surely You have granted him eternal blessings and made him glad with the joy of Your presence. For the king trusts in the LORD; through *the unfailing love of the Most High* he will not be shaken" (Psalm 21:1-7).

Over the years, I became very impressed with the honesty of David in his psalms—honestly describing in one breath his trying and painful circumstances, and yet in the next breath praising the unfailing goodness of God. I have, therefore, made it a practice to *continually* read the Psalms, regardless of what else I may be reading in the Holy Scriptures. As a parting homework assignment for you to do all the remaining days of your life, I want to encourage you to adopt the same practice. Fill your heart with words concerning the goodness of God! Fill your mouth with a testimony to His unfailing love! Speak *this truth*! In the face of everything and anything that may be *true*, speak *the truth of God's goodness and His love*! To those who surround you who are discouraged and faltering and failing, be given to "speaking *the truth* in love" (Eph. 4:15), for "You will know *the truth*, and *the truth* will set you free" (Jn. 8:32). Yes, you will know *Him*, and *He* will set you free (see Jn. 14:6)! Amen!

Taking a Final Step of Faith

*Lord Jesus Christ, You are **the Truth**. I hide myself in You; I cover myself with Your redemptive love!*

*Heavenly Father, You are **the God of truth**. I receive Your unfailing word deep into my heart. I **do** take You at Your word!*

*Blessed Holy Spirit, You are **the Spirit of truth**. I open up my life to Your powerful work within me. Take the things that I have seen on this journey and actualize them within my life. Cause that word to become flesh in me! In Jesus' name. Amen.*

"I will give you the holy and sure blessings promised to David." *Amen!*

Isaiah 55:3 quoted in Acts 13:34

A Concluding Word
From the Author

One of the desires of my heart before the Lord was to have this book published in time for the completion of the new worship and ministry center of Immanuel's Church, the church in which I have been privileged to serve as a pastor these past 12 years. The Lord has graciously granted me my desire!

This book is being released by the publishers in time, not only to be a special memorial to the Lord at the completion of this new "House for His Excellent Glory," but also for the celebration of the twelfth anniversary of Immanuel's Church.

In gratitude my own heart sings with David the meaningful words of this song, written by him "For the dedication of the temple":

> I will exalt you, O LORD,
>> for You lifted me out of the depths ...
> O LORD my God, I called to You for help
>> and You healed me...

Sing to the LORD, you saints of His;
   praise His holy name.
For His anger lasts only a moment,
   but His favor lasts a lifetime;
weeping may remain for a night,
   but rejoicing comes in the morning...

To You, O LORD, I called;
   to the LORD I cried for mercy ...
Hear, O LORD, and be merciful to me;
   O LORD, be my help.

You turned my wailing into dancing;
   You removed my sackcloth and
      clothed me with joy,
that my heart may sing to You and
   not be silent.

O LORD my God, I will give You
   thanks forever.

Psalm 30

Charles P. Schmitt
Immanuel's Church
Fall of 1995

Notes

1. F.B. Meyer, *David: Shepherd, Psalmist, King*, Ft. Washington, PA: Christian Literature Crusade, 1977, p. 54.

2. Alan Redpath, *The Making of a Man of God: Studies in the Life of David*, Old Tappan, NJ: Fleming H. Revell Company, 1962, p. 42.

3. Redpath, p. 67.

4. Mrs. Charles E. Cowman, *Springs in the Valley*, A Cowman Publication, Grand Rapids, MI: Zondervan Publishing House, 1968, p. 200.

5. Ibid.

6. George MacDonald, as quoted in Oswald Chambers' *Not Knowing Wither: The Steps of Abraham's Faith*, London: Simpkin Marshal, Ltd., 1941, p. 51.

7. *The NIV Study Bible*, Kenneth Barker, ed., Grand Rapids, MI: Zondervan Bible Publishers, 1985, p. 906.

8. Watchman Nee (handwritten statement) in Angus I. Kinnear, *Against the Tide: The Story of Watchman Nee*, Ft. Washington, PA: Christian Literature Crusade, 1973, frontispiece.

9. Robert Young, *Young's Literal Translation of the Holy Bible*, Grand Rapids, MI: Baker Book House, 1956, p. 281.

10. *The Interlinear Hebrew/Greek English Bible*, Jay Green, ed. and translator, Vol. 2 (1 Samuel - Psalms), Wilmington, DE: Associated Publishers and Authors, 1976, p. 1103.

11. Meyer, p. 197.

12. Victor Hugo, as quoted in Mrs. Charles E. Cowman, *Streams in the Desert*, Los Angeles, CA: Cowman Publications, 1952, p. 164.

13. Martin J. Selman, *1 Chronicles: An Introduction and Commentary*, Downers Grove, IL: Inter-Varsity Press, 1994, p. 237.

14. Arthur Wallis, *In the Day of Thy Power: The Scriptural Principles of Revival*, Ft. Washington, PA: Christian Literature Crusade, 1961, frontispiece.

15. Beecher, quoted in Mrs. Charles E. Cowman, *Streams in the Desert*, Los Angeles, CA: Cowman Publications, 1952, p. 164.

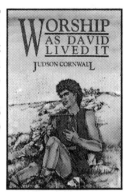
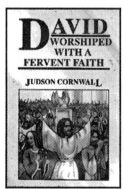

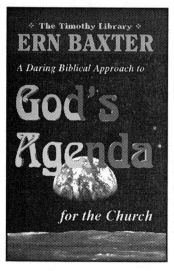
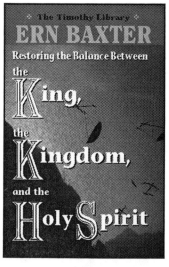

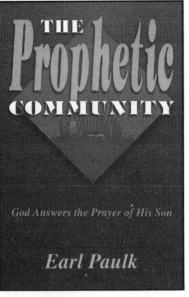

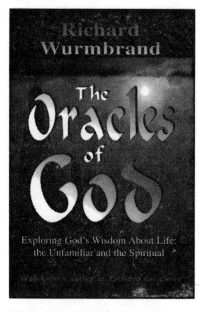

THE ORACLES OF GOD
by Richard Wurmbrand.
Richard Wurmbrand survived the torture and pain of solitary confinement in Soviet prisons and emerged to devote many years to ministering around the world. In *The Oracles of God* this older, battle-scarred pastor passes on his hard-won wisdom to a younger generation.
TPB-196p.
ISBN 1-56043-143-1
Retail $8.99

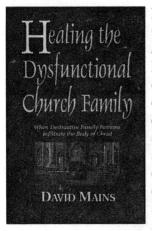

HEALING THE DYSFUNCTIONAL CHURCH FAMILY
by David Mains.

Do Christians automatically shed their dysfunctions at the church door? Of course not. We are just as human in church as we are at home. This profound and honest book calls us to accept one another's humanness—and our tendencies to make mistakes—and explores eight common dysfunctions. Our churches are to be families where we can come and feel loved, helped, and forgiven. Includes small group discussion questions.
TPB-168p. ISBN 1-56043-163-6
Retail $7.99

THE SENSE OF HIS PRESENCE
by David Mains.

What would your church be like on a Sunday morning if Jesus Christ Himself walked through the door? What would happen if God's people really believed He was among them? In this book David Mains discusses eight factors of revival that help us prepare for it and then recognize it when it comes!
TPB-196p.
ISBN 1-56043-162-8
Retail $8.99

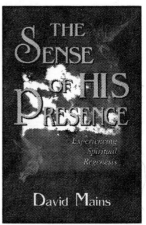

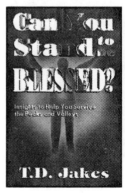